UNDERSTANDING DREAMS

UNDERSTANDING DREAMS

THE GATEWAY TO DREAMS
WITHOUT DREAM INTERPRETATION

MARKKU SIIVOLA
TRANSLATED WITH RICHARD JENKINS

COSIMO BOOKS

NEW YORK

Understanding Dreams: The Gateway to Dreams Without Dream Interpretation
copyright © 2008 by Markku Siivola. First published in Finnish as *Unien opissa—unet itseymmärryksen palveluksessa* by Kirjapaja Publishing House in 2008. Current edition published by Cosimo Books in 2011.

Translated By Richard Jenkins and Markku Siivola.

Cover design by www.popshopstudio.com.
Interior design by www.popshopstudio.com.
Cover image by www.istockphoto.com #4458679

ISBN: 978-1-61640-5489

Cosimo aims to publish books that inspire, inform, and engage readers worldwide. We use innovative print-on-demand technology that enables books to be printed based on specific customer needs. This approach eliminates an artificial scarcity of publications and allows us to distribute books in the most efficient and environmentally sustainable manner. Cosimo also works with printers and paper manufacturers who practice and encourage sustainable forest management, using paper that has been certified by the FSC, SFI, and PEFC whenever possible.

Ordering Information:
Cosimo publications are available at online bookstores. They may also be purchased for educational, business, or promotional use:
Bulk orders: Special discounts are available on bulk orders for reading groups, organizations, businesses, and others.
Custom-label orders: We offer selected books with your customized cover or logo of choice.

For more information, contact us at:

Cosimo, Inc.
P.O. Box 416, Old Chelsea Station
New York, NY 10011

info@cosimobooks.com

or visit us at:
www.cosimobooks.com

TABLE OF CONTENTS

TO THE READER

The *first* aim of this book is to be a *practical guide*, which advises how dreams can be best understood by oneself, with a helper and in a group. We will go through the stages of a dream group process, examining the difficulties that we might encounter on the way, and working out how we can cope with and solve them.

I will describe in detail the dream group process created in Sweden at the beginning of the '70s by a U.S. psychiatry professor emeritus, Montague Ullman. It is the most effective way of studying dreams that I have ever encountered. In this process, dreams belong to the dreamers themselves, instead of to any experts. In dream groups, we will practice *the art of listening,* which enriches our understanding of human relationships and life in general.

The *second* aim of this book is to present the *historical roots* of dream research, which makes it easier to see dreams as one integral sector of the totality of human consciousness, in turn making the modern status of dream research more understandable in our contemporary culture.

The *third* aim is to lead dreams away from their state of isolation by drawing attention to *common features of dream consciousness and waking consciousness*. I will look for these connections in both ordinary everyday experiences, as well as in the final chapter of this book, "Dreams and the Universe," which addresses *philosophies of religions, arts,* and *sciences*. Through all these connections, it is easier to see the common denominator behind varied appearances of human consciousness—the connecting element that permeates ages and cultures—and how dreams are the common language for the whole of mankind. It is in dreams that our humanity is most touchingly visible. It is dreams that offer the opportunity of a deep plunge into the unifying experience of our common, shared human condition.

MY DREAM BACKGROUND

The crucial turning point in my relationship with dreams took place in 1980, when I found a working, functional road to the world of dreams; the road that anyone is able to learn, not only professional therapists. I talk about this experience in detail in "The Tale of Two Telephone Poles." Since then I have guided all kinds of dream groups—first in Sweden in the eighties, later on in Finland—consisting of non-professionals and professional therapists with many kinds of therapeutic orientations. My professional psychiatric dream group activity in Finland began in the early nineties, culminating in 2004 with a weekly training session for psychiatric professionals at the Psychiatric Unit at Jorv Hospital in Southern Finland, which I still conduct today. I maintain that dream group guidance and education is for anyone and everyone, no matter their educational background or dream group experience.

I have combined and modified the dream excerpts in this book from thousands of dreams I have heard. Despite this, they are as representative as original dreams. I have presented only my own dreams as unaltered, albeit in condensed form. Many of my dream examples are certainly more or less familiar. Who hasn't dreamt, for example, of flying, being naked in public places, losing control of their car, missing trains, buses, etc., calling the wrong number, losing their teeth, being in an army or high school examination, or finding new rooms in their house?

THE BASIC CONCEPTS OF THIS BOOK

The basic concepts of my book are *interpretation, explanation, meaning, understanding, and insight.* I use them in a somewhat unusual way. To avoid misunderstandings, I will briefly clarify their definitions here.

Interpretation and explanation of dreams

If you cannot understand a foreign language, you need an interpreter. However, the interpretation process always misses and distorts some of the original meaning. This happens in dream interpretation, too, which more or less twists the original nature of dreams, squeezing them into the interpretative mold defined by the respective interpretation system. Rather than resorting to using any interpreter, a much better solution is to learn the foreign language personally. Only then is it possible to understand the living nuances it contains.

Explaining dreams is closely related to *interpreting* dreams, but explanations do not contain as much autocratic unfounded self-confidence as dream interpretations. These two concepts are so closely related that they are used interchangeably in most cases.

I address the broader connections between interpretation and pre-conceptions, assumptions, and prejudices on page 19.

The meaning of dreams

Both interpretation and explanation tell us what a dream *means.* Most interpretation systems are content with this initial, surface explanation. That is not enough. This book aims to understand dreams on a deeper level, rather than simply discovering what the dream might *mean.* With their seeming clarity, *meanings* may be able to calm down our restlessness at our inability to confront face to face the big questions of life. The meaning found in the dream is not yet "being inside" the dream. The meaning is not yet intimate, lacking a vivid understanding, but is a distant, predominantly intelligence-oriented outside view, a shadow of the original experience. Meanings may be very pleasing because of their fine-looking logicality, which seems to explain the dream nicely, but the logical compatibility does not necessarily have anything to do with the living, true content of the dream. The sign of the deeper opening of any dream is not intellectual satisfaction caused by the discovery of meaning, but the dreamer's emotional reaction; the impact of an aha! moment (the bodily gut feeling that accompanies sudden insight). This reaction will not happen if the only thing we are seeking is a simple meaning.

Understanding and insight of dreams

Insight into the nature of dreams cannot be attained through interpretations and explanations, but through immersive dedication to dreams. No explanation can exhaustively define the infinite nature of dreams. It is not difficult to understand that interpreting a sunset would be quite unreasonable, or on the other hand, *too* reasonable. Squeezing a sunset into explanations about physical phenomena is of course a very rational activity, in some circumstances even producing useful results, but explanations can never catch the feeling that is awakened in us, penetrating our whole being, when we are watching the spectacle of cosmic art flaming in the horizon.

The same is valid with regard to the artistic quality of dreams. Every night we surpass our limits by creating a work of art, which is unattainable by our daytime imagination. It is true that we are able to explain dreams with the help of innumerable dream interpretation systems, exactly like an art historian is able to make *Mona Lisa* fit into his cultural history interpretation, but these kinds of interpretations and explanations do not help us to personally experience or understand a realization of ourselves and life in general through the art of our own dreams.

PRACTICE ABOVE ALL

The practical guide to understanding dreams begins on page 69. If this guide is not tested in practice, this book is like reading the menu without tasting the meal. You can only discover the real taste of dreams by experiencing it personally.

I will talk about the possibilities and difficulties that dreamers encounter when trying to understand dreams, first alone, which is the most difficult way, and then with a helper, which is a bit easier. Finally, I will talk about understanding dreams with small groups, which are the most effective in dream work.

My goal is to inspire the reader to form a dream group, or to visit groups arranged by others, because *the small groups presented in this book are the most effective tools to understand the language of dreams.*

So-called experiential dream groups are based on the dream group process, which Professor Montague Ullman developed. These groups do not use dreams as stepping-stones to other topics outside dreams, but use all their energy and time to plunge with all their senses into dreams like a diver into water, letting the dream surround them completely, experiencing it with all their senses, being immersed in it and getting a first-hand experience of it instead of theorizing about it on the seashore. *The essential feature of the dream group process is that it contains neither any dream interpretation system nor any dream interpretation authority. The dream group leader may be the expert in knowing the dream group process, but not the expert of any particular dream.*

Specific care is taken to ensure that the dreamer always has the last word in what the dream means *to the dreamer personally.* Thus, dreams are returned from dream experts to those whom they really belong: the dreamers themselves.

BEYOND DREAMS

Dreams are not the only road to Rome!

While writing this book I experienced a number of dreams, revealing how I had to search constantly for the delicate balance that could convey the importance of dreams and at the same time warn about worshipping dreams too much. No doubt dreams and dream groups may be useful tools for our waking life, but they are not an end in and of themselves.

> *I dream that it has been publicly announced that I will marry a woman sitting outside. I glance out of the window. Lo and behold, there really is a woman, sitting there on a bench, waiting for something! I think that I must immediately go to her and clear up this mess. How can it be possible that I have promised to marry a total stranger?*

The night preceding the dream, I had felt considerable anxiety about taking part in a certain dream group, which functioned inadequately. But I was unable to avoid it because I had made a contract to lead that group. I felt the same kind of aversion to the woman in my dream as I felt towards my dysfunctional dream group in the "real world." I felt that the group expected something from me that I was incapable of delivering, and similarly, in my dream, I had promised the woman too much. In a way, I was letting dreams dominate my life. I was beginning to feel that I was married to dreams! There was a desire to de-idolize dreams, to soften my role as a dream authority, because my role now threatened to engulf me. But my unhappy marriage with this dysfunctional dream group was already a fact. I could not break with it; I simply had to live with it.

To sell oneself too deeply to only one idea, such as dreams, is mental prostitution. But how on earth would I be able to find the right balance? How would I tell about the profoundness and beauty of dreams without overselling them?

And yet, in spite of all these contradictions, I have to confess that the method presented in this book is the best I have found. It is the only approach to dreams that does not awaken ideological claustrophobia in me. It is a way devised from the ground up to be used by anybody, regardless of beliefs for or against it. Who knows if tomorrow I will find another, better way, but so far, the dream group method is the best I have seen. I think I am still married with my dream girl.

I also dreamt about a very *real* girl of my dreams, about my wife:

> *I turned onto the crossroad from the road, which goes by my child-hood house. It proved to be the wrong way. I tried to go back, but it was troublesome. I was worried. My wife had not turned onto this crossroad but had continued directly onward. She waited for me at some distance.*

When I woke up, the feeling of the dream was the same feeling I had the whole day before. My wife had just completed her own book, ready to be delivered to the publisher. On the same day, I had completed a considerable part of my manuscript, but I had not found a way to continue. I had anxiously reflected on this the whole day, trying to continue my writing in various directions, but none seemed to be *my* direction. I had to *reverse* my direction. The road going by my childhood house, the road that my wife had chosen and walked to the end of, is named *Pirjo's Road*. My wife's name is *Pirjo*. She had advanced to the end of the road of her own book, *waiting* for me to follow her, if only I could find *my road*. However, the very same childhood road of mine was also Pirjo's Road, the common, uniting road for both of us.

After all this, I have to take back my own words once more, stating that there are *no* roads to the deepest understanding of the most essential things. No dream roads, no other roads, either. Nothing more is needed than *truthfulness*—and what this truthfulness is, is completely beyond any explanation. Every one of us knows what it is, but we do not always want to know. We can advance very far on the road of dreams, into our souls. But then even this dream road ends.

The remaining part of the road is the *roadless road*. To travel down this road is a journey we must make completely alone, without the support of road signs, instructions, therapies, conceptual systems, formal religions, dreams, or dream groups. We are bound to continue our travel aided only by our truthfulness, stumbling, groping, fumbling toward our own, most genuine self.

Martin Buber wrote in *Ich und Du* (I and Thou):"All the prescriptions that have been excogitated and invented in the ages of human spirit, all the preparations, exercises and meditations that have been suggested, have nothing to do with the primally simple fact of encounter."[1]

CHAPTER ONE

FREQUENTLY ASKED QUESTIONS ABOUT DREAMS

WHAT IS THE IMPORTANCE OF PSYCHOANALYSIS TO THE UNDERSTANDING OF DREAMS?

Attempts to take dreams seriously and to understand them, not merely as entertainment, are still strongly chained to psychoanalysis. Freud's pioneering work with dreams has been an enormous service to the appreciation and awareness of dreams in Western culture, and is actually the greatest advancement in the history of dream research. On the other hand, even with all the positive factors the psychoanalytic dream view contains, it also contains factors which impede dream understanding. Psychoanalysis does not help us to attain the practical goal for which this book is aiming: bringing dream understanding from behind the closed doors of psychotherapy to within reach of any non-professional for the benefit of self-understanding. This book touches on psychoanalysis only in areas limited to dreams, not in the many other areas which psychoanalysis embraces. My view touches only the mainstream of psychoanalysis, originating directly from Freud himself, *not* from the derivative trends born during later decades.

DO DREAMS HAVE ANY SENSE AT ALL?

No. They are senseless. Our sensible rationality leaves us when we are falling asleep— fortunately—whereupon our intellect does not have a chance to practice its intrigues and excuses. Because of this our dreams express our true feelings so openly.

How come openly? I do not understand even the slightest bit of them, and in addition to lacking any sense, they do not seem to contain any feelings either.

Dreams are full of feelings, which you passed over when you were awake for one reason or another. When you begin to reflect on your dream after awakening, you do it with the same waking consciousness that triggered the dream in the first place. You need time and concentrated attention, often with the help of others, in order to find new ways of looking at your dreams and learning to listen to life in a way which opens to you richer vistas.

At first the language of dreams seems to be foreign. If you do not understand Chinese, you know that the fault does not lie with the language, but because you have not mastered it. It is useless to demand that dreams use the language of our waking consciousness. Instead, it is our waking consciousness which must learn and listen to the emotion-based language of dreams. The more you learn the pictorial language of dreams, the more you appreciate the intensity of their expression in your life. Only the finest poetry is able to approximate the truthfulness of the dream. The poet, novelist, essayist, and movie scriptwriter Jim Harrison writes in his anthology *Just Before Dark* (1991):

"Poetry at its best is the language your soul would speak if you could teach your soul to speak."

ARE PEOPLE INTERESTED IN THEIR OWN DREAMS CRAZY?

Massive amounts of dream worship literature impose on dreams an over-appreciated value and glory, or trivialize them with oversimplified symbol lists. The abundance of this literature and the shortage of higher-level dream information tell us that dreams do not have any serious foothold at all among the values typical for Western societies. People who love to tell their own dreams to almost anybody seem often to be uncritical victims of sentimentality and all kinds of esoteric secret doctrines. Thus it is no wonder that dreams are often associated with foolishness. The purpose of this book is to help the reader dig up something more essential buried under these pre-digested superficialities.

CAN DREAM INTERPRETATION BE HARMFUL?

Yes. Dream *interpretation* can be harmful, whereas dream *appreciation* cannot. I return later to the harmful connotations of interpretation and to possibilities of understanding one's own dreams in ways other than via interpretation. For the present I state only that when an interpreter believes he knows better than the dreamer what a dream means, and if the interpreter happens to own a considerable amount of expert authority and lack of consideration, he may be capable of harming the dreamer. Authority that subjugates another human being is always harmful, irrespective of whether it presents itself disguised as dream interpretation or as some other form of self-important, know-all-attitude. Appreciating dreams, on the other hand, is an integrating, unifying experience.

IN WHAT WAY CAN UNDERSTANDING DREAMS BE BENEFICIAL FOR ME?

Understanding dreams can help individuals in many ways. One example is that it can rescue your marriage, even lift it to a higher level than ever before. I am one of those lucky ones who have had the opportunity to experience it personally.

The more you understand the world of dream images, the more you will see how the inner world of images affects us continually— during the day as well as at night. You will gain greater sensitivity and understand *everything*, including how the inner world of images is appearing: in poetry, paintings, music, fantasies, fairytales, myths, religions, and in illusions and hallucinations. You'll better understand your fellow man and yourself, wherever you may meet, and whatever your common interests may be. Understanding dreams brings along the art of listening, listening to wholeness, not only to mere words. One who is guided only by intellect and reasoning drifts more easily into difficulties in life than one who is able to sense the whole range of emotions more delicately. The happiness of our lives is greatly dependent on understanding the levels of our emotional and mental imagery.

What special status do dreams have in this process of understanding each other's emotions? Dreams are the purest form of all mental images, the first ancestors of other pictorial forms, having least distance from the truth. They are the most unselfish and most authentic images of our lives. Other mental images are derivatives of these. We can, of course, study ourselves with the help of these derivatives as well, the most obvious being the multitude of art forms. Thus, dreams are not the only gate to the depths of our minds, and there is no sense in sacrificing our time exclusively to the study of dreams. Dreams are the most straightforward, but at times, undeniably complicated, because they represent dimensions of our minds, which our waking consciousness is able to approach only with great difficulty. Their incomprehensibility may extinguish our enthusiasm, frustrating us.

But I feel my life is quite OK. My human relations are alright, and I don't need anything extra in my life.

Congratulations on your good luck and successful choices! Dreams are not the only way to have a good life. Why study them if you feel that you do not need them? Dreams *do* contain more information about yourself than you believe, but it might well be that lessons you learn on the other paths during your journey through life will be more suitable for you than any dream studies. You might even become too dependent on dreams. Dream fanaticism among many other forms of extremism is not an unknown phenomenon. There are enough salesmen peddling all kinds of dogmas in the present-day deluge of information, so there really are reasons for maintaining a critical attitude.

IS IT POSSIBLE FOR EVERYONE TO LEARN TO UNDERSTAND DREAMS?

No. There are many individuals for whom it realistically won't be possible due to physical and psychological obstacles. The great majority of people, however, do have potential for understanding dreams in theory, but not in practice.

Many people with fully satisfactory learning capabilities could be interested in dreams, but because they have not succeeded in finding a suitable method for understanding dreams, their interest fades at square one. Some people are not able to remember their dreams, despite great effort. For some people, the obstacle consists of the difficulty in understanding the symbolic nuances of language. This places restraints on one's acquaintance with not only dreams, but also poetry.

No one, not even those of us equipped with the most sensitive intuitive abilities, is able to understand dreams completely, be they one's own or others' dreams. The more you learn to understand dreams, the more you will notice that even after many insights, they still contain something more you are not able to understand. Dreams are, in their multidimensional boundlessness, too immense to be understood completely and are beyond the grasp of our waking life consciousness.

DO CLAIRVOYANT AND PRECOGNITIVE DREAMS EXIST?

Many believe in them. Many do not. Belief and disbelief in them are useless, because both attitudes are dead ends, perpetually inflamed topics for never-ending argumentation for and against, in a way where open-minded exploration has been pushed away. My opinion about them does not advance the main purpose of my book: to guide people to better understand their own dreams and their whole life. That's why I have to abandon this topic at this time.

CHAPTER TWO

IN SEARCH OF THE MEANING OF DREAMS

OUR NIGHTLY COMPANIONS

Sleeping takes up one third of our lives. Because one person dreams about one and half hours per night, we can calculate that the total dreaming time for our human race of almost seven billion inhabitants totals more than a million years per night.

What is this nightly phenomenon, which may influence so strongly our feelings on the following day, like the slowly lingering morning mist above the landscape? Is it empty insignificance or filled with deep meaning? Is it merely the nightly background noise of our restless brains or the voices of angels? Is it useless, nonsensical fooling around in dream landscapes, evolved from the ape? Is it an unnecessary remnant like our appendix, or the pictorial language of some higher consciousness which we need to understand?

Freud's famous contemporary, the American psychologist William James, considered dreams to be an independent type of reality. He said in *The Principles of Psychology*: "But if a dream haunts us and compels our attention during the day it is very apt to remain figuring in our consciousness as a sort of sub-universe alongside of the waking world. Most people have probably had dreams which it is hard to imagine not to have been glimpses into an actually existing region of being."[2]

In the course of the day, the emotional waves evoked by dreams begin to subside, the watery surface of living smoothes down, and the monsters sent from the unknown depths of even the worst nightmares withdraw under the surface of waking consciousness, waiting there for the next night.

Most of us have at least in some stage of our lives tried to explore our own dreams. Some have reflected on dreams since childhood and their thirst for knowledge has pushed them in an attempt to untangle them. For some they are enchanting, containing recognizable elements despite their bizarreness. Some lock them away as too disquieting in the back rooms of their minds. Some are reminded of the horrors of living, when a shocking dream has torn the curtain of consciousness in half, stomping on it with vigor, signaling how miserably frail the conscious self is in the grip of the giants of the dream. Only for very few have dreams become significant companions in everyday life.

Obstacles in the seeker's way

Dreams are the deepest images of our inner visions. The influence of our day consciousness is not able to distort them, unlike their derivative images, which flow in the channels of folklore, fairytales, myths, religions, and art forms. Seldom does dream interpretation literature guide readers to the source of their innermost self, diverting them to unimaginative routine external answers instead. Typical dream handbooks are near relatives of horoscopes, mostly entertaining attempts to peek into something more exciting than everyday life. "Tell me, stars and dreams, if I will hit the jackpot, get married, if he/she is the right one for me." On the other hand, there is psychotherapeutic literature emphasizing years of psychotherapy research studies as the only way to understand dreams. As a consequence, the dream seeker finds it difficult to explore dreams in any direction. Some people have the energy to maintain a dream diary, but as a solitary interest, over the course of time, it tends to lay forgotten in the most remote corner of a bookshelf.

Serious seekers practically never find serious support for their interest among best friends, co-workers, or family members. The coffee break is perhaps the most common setting for dream chatter, but it is restrained by its own invisible regulations, which forbid taking dreams too seriously. Beneath the surface of small talk flows the undercurrent of our mutual fear of each other, which must not be revealed by indulging in controversially serious topics, as good conduct guides have always known. We bump into the same, almost invisible resistance against dreams everywhere, sometimes expressed as ridicule, sometimes as worry from loved ones over the crazy dream lover. "Please-do-not-confuse-your-mind-with-that-kind-of-nonsense" type comments are beginning to appear in more and more serious tones.

Our helplessness in dealing with dreams is sadly most visible between close friends. Even if we trust each other, and even if we, through the years, would have gathered around serious topics about life and living, and even if everybody had been interested in dreams, reflecting on them remains almost without substance, because nobody knows how to proceed. If we were to dig out some old, forgotten dream dictionaries from our bookshelves, and if we played with their symbol lists a while, most of us realize their worthlessness. Even Freud cannot help, because not even he offered such methods which were realistically applicable in the hands of non-professionals.

Modern culture, which appreciates hard, explicit knowledge and scientific evidence, is a poor breeding ground for dreams. Dreams find their place in it only in a sanitized form as the results of analytical research, as fish pulled out of the water of our subconscious mind and left to die on shore. They still have the shape of the fish, but are no longer alive. In this culture, dreams have been excluded even from domains where one would think that they could be massively utilized: within psychiatry and psychotherapies. The regrettable fact is that psychiatry and even many psychotherapy orientations, are dream deserts, where dreams are found flattened by interpretations in theoretical herbaria, not as living blossoms.

THE KEYS TO MY OWN EXPLORATION

My own exploration began when I was about ten years old. I had a presentiment about the existence of something that I eagerly wanted to know, but I could not yet understand what it might be.

The only serious form of exploring the world, which I found at that time, was scientific exploration. It was the only one which, in my opinion, had an inbuilt capacity to regenerate, to learn from its own mistakes, and to approach reality better than religions that are stuck in their own standard liturgies. Eager to learn, I glued newspaper articles about scientific topics in my scrapbook. I loved chemistry and physics and wrote only about science in every Finnish language composition. My teacher finally forbade me from continuing to write only about natural sciences after I had managed to turn even the composition named "No smoke without fire" into a scientific composition by writing about fire in the hearts of scientists, which then produces the smoke of scientific discoveries.

But something was missing. At that time I felt an urge to write compositions about topics that were outside the natural sciences and out of the reach of rational intellect. I was unable to write because I still could not understand what it was all about in my mind when even science did not seem to be enough. I simply could not find any words for this inner urge.

Ten more years passed. When I was in my twenties I at last found what turned out to be the most important prerequisite for my dream exploration. The crucial moment came when I was reading a book I had borrowed, compiled from talks by the late Jiddu Krishnamurti. I did not know what kind of man he was, but this book, which by chance I had come across in the library, appeared interesting. When people asked him the usual questions about truth and love and humanity that have occupied human minds through the ages, he always pointed out how the question itself indicated that the questioner did not want to abandon the unproductive state of mind which prevented him from finding the real answer, found only inside the questioner, not from any outside person. "Your question indicates that you do not want to know!" I was irritated by that answer; it felt like an insult to the poor questioner.

But I looked at his assertion once more, even though I felt it was extremely arrogant. This time it caught my attention. I kept staring at it, and suddenly the dam broke, and all the questions that had grown behind it in my mind over the last decade came flooding out.

"Your question indicates that you do not want to know!"

How clear, how simple this truth really was! This was the truth I had sensed since my childhood, but only now it transformed into the personally experienced knowledge that the way to life's basic questions must be found completely alone, on the road which has no road signs and no predefined destination, because truth is a pathless land, and only truthfulness can lead us to where we already are.

This moment vaccinated me against dream interpretation diseases. Only the dreamer can really understand his own dream, nobody else. Interpreters simply cannot ever be right.

I had not yet quite understood the magnitude of my discovery concerning dreams. However, this flash of insight had already illuminated the significance of the inner way and the ever-present danger of falling to the mercy of external opinions.

Still fifteen more years were needed before I, at age 35, found a nonviolent path to the realm of dreams. Only then did the flash of my earlier experience enter into the service of dream exploration.

This is how it happened:

THE TALE OF TWO TELEPHONE POLES

It was the autumn of 1980 in Boden, a little town in Northern Sweden. I was working as a psychiatrist when I heard my co-workers talking about a psychoanalyst who was coming to lead a dream group. They asked if I was interested, and I said "No!"

I reacted so negatively because for fear of reliving the intense claustrophobia I had experienced during my years in psychiatry training when, according to my teachers, every oblong, elongated object symbolized a penis and every bowl-like formation, a vagina. Why should this psychoanalyst be any different?

I remembered an embarrassing situation that happened in the early days of my medical training during the first psychiatry meeting I ever attended. I arrived late, sat down, and tried to get into the discussion. For a while I thought I had come into the wrong room, because the behavior of my older colleagues was so strange.

For a moment I thought that they might be rehearsing an odd burlesque play, perhaps for a personnel party. Everyone was extremely serious, talking about the mother's breast in a way that made the situation so absurd, that with all my inexperience, I really believed they were joking!

Then they changed the topic. Now soil symbolized a vagina and a hoe, the penis which penetrates it. I still remember my acute embarrassment and anxiety over hiding my bewilderment, when it began to dawn on me that these gentlemen were seriously serious! They did not pop out of their theorizing, but continued to exist as though in a theoretical bubble, sealed from life outside, seeing only their own intellectual projections on the walls of that bubble, not the world outside.

The claustrophobic experiences continued throughout my studies but, fortunately, only a couple of them were as grotesque as this first encounter with traditional psychoanalytic thinking. During the years of my medical studies, I became more and more conscious of the devastating effect of placing life into the Procrustean bed of conceptual systems, whatever their nature. I began to recognize that whatever the system, it always acts as a filter between the observer and the observed, diluting the artistry of life.

My fellow workers in Boden did not give up on pressing me to attend the dream group, and at last, I gave in. This decision turned out to be one of the most important turning points of my life.

During the first day of the workshop, my strange feeling about the leader of the group, Montague "Monte" Ullman, grew stronger. This man did not interpret anything, but, in an extremely gentle way I had never seen before, guided the group to listen to dreams. I saw for the first time how the dream opened into its full glory, speaking with its own voice to the whole group.

There was something in him, something I recognized deeply inside myself, some similarity, some indefinable connection, some resonance. Longing for something long ago forgotten and lost, I recognized a living force inside me, a spark of energy I had always been after, something beyond all explanation and theory. I saw this man catch the uncatchable, creating an atmosphere where the dream was able to bloom in all its touching innocence.

And how different we still were, he and I! I was young, he was old; I spoke English hesitantly and he was fluent; we were from different cultures, living on opposite sides of the earth. But all these differences could not explain away the common factor. He was a stranger to me and at the same time, he was not.

The second day of the dream group dawned. Monte asked if anyone had a dream to share, but no one did. He then said he had one. It was a short sequence, and it was about me:

In his dream, I had come to his hotel room and asked two questions, which he did not remember, nor did he remember his answer to the first one. The answer to the second one was this: he took me to the window of his hotel room, and pointed at two telephone poles outside. He said to me, "If you understand why those telephone poles are just there and nowhere else, you have received the answer to your questions."

That was Monte's dream, and the turning point for me. Monte said he did not know the message of the dream. But I did. The dream immediately opened to me. The opening was not a logical process, but a strong immediate emotional impact. The dream symbolized perfectly the intriguing feeling I had about Monte the previous day. There we were, Monte and I, like two telephone poles, irrevocably apart, without any possibility to come closer to one another. Just as I had felt it the day before! But between the two poles there was an electrical unifying current. Just as I had felt it the day before!

The dream said that if I understood the position of the poles I had received the answer. I understood, and received the answer, just like the dream said I would!

The dream was his, not mine. How could I know if my view of the metaphors was right or wrong? It was irrelevant. Right and wrong belong to the realm of the rational world where dreams cannot be understood. The flashing impact opened me to the living view about the potential of dreams. The dream illuminated much more clearly the feelings that I had been unable to understand on my own.

The last act of this dream was played out twenty years later. I had been busy for some months building up Monte's website, scanning hundreds of pages of material, which Monte kept sending me by fax. One night my wife said, "Now the dream has really come true," pointing to the way Monte and I communicated: we, the two telephone poles, were there again, the connective current of faxes flowing through the telephone lines between us, now across the globe! Then I felt that the dream had at last conveyed its contents at all levels.

Right or wrong? Was it a coincidence or was Monte's dream precognitive? I do not care. I can never know. I know that the dream does contain more, like all dreams; they are limitless like life itself, and not everything they contain can ever be grasped completely.

Either way, this incident gave me at last the key to dreams, which has helped me maintain my faith in the incorruptible core of all human beings, irrespective of how deeply it may have been buried behind the barriers we put up against each other in our daily struggle of existence. Dreams have been the oasis of innocence, the purity of the human soul during my journey through the desert of everyday routines and the overemphasis of our separateness from each other in the competitive atmosphere of our culture.

Dreams are the common realm, the connective, healing tissue for those of us who have lost our way to the connectedness of the human species.

> *You'll find him without any search*
> *when you will find yourself*
> *when you see in dearest friend*
> *your own soul, nothing else*
> *when you see that even he*
> *has happiness not found*
> *and see how he, alongside you*
> *has equal pain around.*[3]

CHAPTER THREE

FROM DREAM INTERPRETATION TO DREAM APPRECIATION

IN SEARCH OF DREAM INTERPRETATION

Dream interpretation has been practiced from the beginning of history in all cultures, and the status of interpreters in cultural and political circles has varied through the centuries. Interpretations have stayed close to religion—understandable due to the religious imagery dreams often contain—and they continue to do so because of the unusually powerful, even life-changing religious experiences dreams trigger.

The oldest dream interpretation manual is a papyrus scroll from Egypt dating between 1700 and 2000 B.C.[4,5] The most well-known ancient dream interpreter is certainly Artemidorus Daldianus, famed for the dream book he wrote two thousand years ago.[6] He was convinced about the superiority of his dream interpretation system. It cannot be denied that he keenly understood the connection between dream symbols and the dreamer's life situation and culture.

In the Western countries, religion has not been the most suitable channel to awaken interest in dreams. A mode of thought that valued scientific thinking swiftly gained strength in the last century. It was well-suited to a rational approach to dreams, offered by Sigmund Freud (1856–1939), who broke the dream bank in 1899 with his work *The Interpretation of Dreams.* Freud called his approach to dreams an *interpretation,* and because of his very strong influence, this *interpretation* concept rose to unparalleled power. This concept has adhered to dreams so tightly, that these two words can be separated from each other only by brute force. The French translator of Freud's works, philosopher and psychoanalyst Jean-Bertrand Pontalis has made similar remarks[7]:

> Freud's book *Die Traumdeutung* (1900): the title itself already links, indeed irrevocably unites, the dream and its interpretation. Freud, at the same time as he totally revises it, places himself in the tradition of the various seers, secular and religious, where the dream is consecrated to its meaning, thus to some extent neglecting the dream as experience.[8]

Is it possible to approach dreams productively in any way other than by interpreting them? Freud's influence on us is such that Freudian interpretation, as a young cuckoo, seems to have pushed all other serious approaches to dreams out of the nest. Interpretation has been rooted so firmly into our language that people who already have learned to avoid dream interpretation may still, out of habit, use this word when they mean some non-interpretive approach to dreams instead.

As every word has many nuances which may even be contradictory to each other depending on their context, we have to go into defining the very essence of interpretation—not only dream interpretation, but interpretation in a broader sense.

Psychoanalytic view of interpretation

Dream interpretation is only one area where interpretation can be practiced. Understanding the broader meaning of interpretation also helps to better understand the variety of nuances contained in dream interpretation. Veikko Tähkä, the Grand Old Man of Finnish psychoanalysis, wrote in his work *Mind and Its Treatment: A Psychoanalytic Approach* that the traditional concept of "interpretation" is the analyst's verbal expression, meant to bring mental conflicts that were previously unconscious to the patient's awareness.[9] Interpretation is the primary tool, a tank that rumbles over the weakest point in a patient's defenses at an exactly chosen, strategic moment where it will do the most damage. This classical psychoanalytic concept of interpretation contains to some degree the "battle of wits" where the analyst strives to maintain the upper hand. It is thus a contest between opposing forces. Freud states this in his lecture *Resistance and Repression*: "Indeed we come finally to understand that the overcoming of these resistances is the essential function of analysis."[10]

While for decades analysts have expanded their professional field to include therapy for patients who have deeper mental disturbances than neuroses, this development has made the whole concept of interpretation more diffused and obscured. Consequently, many other procedures in the analyst's arsenal of methods may be called interpretation, like confrontation, clarification, and empathic description (comparable to parents, who have a good understanding of their children and make it known to them). Even rational information may sometimes be called interpretation.

The historical burden of interpretation

The long-standing influence of psychoanalysis on dreams has created a prototype image of dream interpretation in the eyes of both professionals and non-professionals: The *dream interpreter is an academically trained psychotherapist, especially a psychoanalyst, who understands the dreamer's dreams better than the dreamer. Because of his authority, he is able to have the last word despite the dreamer's own view about his dreams.*

By psychoanalysis, I mean only the *general gestalt of its historical main course*, originating from Freud, not its later tributaries or any other particular psychoanalyst, unless specifically mentioned otherwise.

Those who do not master a foreign language need an interpreter. An interpreter is therefore more skilled than the one who needs him. He is the professional, the expert at his language. This kind of view is simple-mindedly applied to dream interpretation as well: the interpreter of dreams is able to translate dream language to the waking consciousness language better than his less-skilled client. If the interpreter is a psychoanalyst, he has acquired his interpreting authority *automatically* as part of the *general* authority of his profession, regardless of his own individual skills. Because of the standing of the psychoanalytic profession, the concept of interpretation has become implanted deeply in Western culture.

The corresponding construction to psychoanalysis is depicted especially richly and brilliantly in Nobel writer Hermann Hesse's novel *The Glass Bead Game*. It tells the story of a carefully isolated autonomous elite province Castalia, where an intellectually high-level, ethereal brotherhood is playing and refining the enormous, perpetual game, consisting of sciences and arts, to more and more complex syntheses. It is a "safe, high-level, iron-clad, inherently logical theoretical system, capable of converting disbelievers back to the care of the brotherhood and rejecting the external criticism."[11]

Concerning the value of psychoanalysis, it has intentionally avoided, especially during the first decades of its existence, evaluations from other scientific disciplines, taking care not to apply to itself any other criteria than its own. Because of this, its conceptual system has retained its internal coherence relatively well, but, on the other hand, it has isolated itself from the rest of the world. It has kept itself as a Castalian-like bulletproof system, endowing its members with a belief more or less founded by their own individual talents. As Tähkä states in his aforementioned book: "One's own role as a superior judge of human nature is not, as is well known, a completely unknown character trait in many analysts and psychotherapists— aging analyst's narcissistic defenses which have been preserved and with age pronounced, may make him increasingly pretentious in analytic societies."

The charm of psychoanalysis appeals to civilized rationalists; to a typical product of our hard-fact-loving contemporary culture. They may long for deeper knowledge about the abysses of the human mind, but dare to descend to its depths on only the strong rope of all-explaining theory. This kind of exploration may yield significant information about the human psyche; on the other hand, it compresses its findings, including dreams, into the matrix of unchangeable concepts, which impoverishes the original vitality of these findings.

The first article about Finnish psychoanalysis was published as early as 1910. Not until the '50s did psychoanalysis flourish in Finland and enjoy popularity for a few decades. In the '80s, almost all professors in Finnish psychiatry were also psychoanalysts. Even though the status of psychoanalysis in psychiatry is no longer as elevated, it still makes an appearance every now and then in the media as an unresolved wrestling match between its defenders and opponents.

Interpretation, presupposition and prejudice

Our daily communication is limited by many obstacles, such as etiquette, good manners, and traditions. We stay inside these limitations almost automatically without even noticing them. These limiting boundaries force our communication into empty small talk, into standardized communication vocabulary, making superficial, easy contacts possible; however, it also affords a chance to avoid establishing deeper relationships. These boundaries protect us, but they confine us to straitjackets. Without these boundaries, most of us are vulnerable and weak, like tortoises torn out of their shells. Thus, they are necessary, good or bad.

Who wouldn't long for more realistic, more truthful encounters? But being successful in them is a question of craft and talent and the general tools offered by our culture hardly help in developing these skills. Therefore, we tend to stay timidly at a polite distance from each other. The missing holes in our knowledge about each other fill up with suppositions, which tend to freeze into presuppositions and harden into prejudices.

In our everyday lives, interpretation is often manifested as presuppositions, with which we substitute and complement our observations. The limitations of our perception, including *biological* limits, compel us to simplify reality by classifying it into more controllable, smaller entities. As error-prone as the simplifying operations may be, we have needed them in the course of evolution to survive both individually and as groups. In the face of impending danger, we may have to decide in a fraction of a second which class the menace belongs to: friend or foe? The immediate interpretation of this situation may even save us from death.

The tragic side of interpretation can be seen in classifications of nations and groups, especially ethnic, when we interpret individuals to represent their whole reference group before we have had time to become acquainted with them.

Then we use our interpretations in a way that leads us astray in the interpretation of dreams, as well, when we suppose that we can re-apply standard meanings learned earlier to present situations.

The more we become aware of our automatic culture-based interpretations, the more realistic our chances to really understand the truer essence of our fellow human beings, including dreams that lead to increased understanding and that diminish our need to hide from each other behind our various roles, become.

DREAM APPRECIATION

As a young psychoanalyst, Montague Ullman, a U.S. psychiatrist and psychoanalyst, became increasingly uncomfortable with the nuances in the expression *dream interpretation*. In the 1950s he heard psychoanalyst Marianne Horney Eckardt use the expression, which caught the essence of dream work (note: Ullman's dream work concept is completely different from the one Freud used). Ullman wrote, "She eschewed the term *dream interpretation* when applied to the dream. She felt it was too restrictive and that it tended to pigeon-hole something that flowed through any interpretive net meant to catch it. She felt that *dream appreciation* was a more felicitous way of describing the nature of the engagement of patient and therapist."[12] Ullman adopted this expression immediately and used it from then on.

In this book, I use the terms *appreciation* and *understanding* almost interchangeably, the difference being that with understanding I mean a completely *neutral* attitude to dreams, whereas appreciation has a *positive* connotation.

The noted psychoanalyst Erich Fromm (1900–1980) states that in the subtitle of his book *The Forgotten language—an Introduction to the Understanding of Dreams, Fairytales and Myths*, he chose the term *understanding* instead of *interpretation:* "The term, an introduction to the understanding of dreams, etc., was chosen intentionally instead of using the more conventional term interpretation. [...] The problem is indeed one of understanding it rather than of interpreting as if one dealt with an artificially manufactured secret code."[13]

Fromm also noted:

> *Interpretation of dreams is still considered legitimate only when employed by the psychiatrist in the treatment of neurotic patients. On the contrary, I believe that symbolic language is the one foreign language that each of us must learn. Its understanding brings us in touch with one of the most significant sources of wisdom, that of the myth, and it brings us in touch with the deeper layers of our own*

personalities. In fact, it helps us to understand a level of experience that is specifically human because it is that level which is common to all humanity, in content as well as in style.

The precondition for insightful understanding of dreams is safety. Interpretations by their very nature add to the dreamer's resistance. Anything threatening to his safety must be minimized as much as possible. Ullman-type dream groups contain many safety measures, which protect the dreamer very effectively from interpretations and confrontations of any kind. This may give the impression that no one is allowed to say much of anything about the dream. Quite the contrary! When all threats around the dreamer are minimized, he can lower his protective bulwark and quit censoring every word, letting the description of the dream flow unhampered, more immediately and from deeper layers of the psyche. The more he is encouraged, the more his story transforms into a picturesque and emotional narration that creates multi-dimensional *visions* in addition to getting from point A to point B, advancing one-dimensional chains of thought. This raises the odds of everyone in the group attaining an insightful understanding of the dream.

Unlearning

Ullman worked sixteen years as a traditional psychoanalyst before he switched to the development work of his own dream group process. He found this process to be the most potent way of understanding the mental core of another human being. He noted that patients' resistance to interpretation was only partly caused by patients and partly by the psychoanalytic approach itself. The patient experienced it as an invasion attempt, which it in fact proved to be, despite its well-meaning purpose. This finding caused Ullman to abandon the psychoanalytic approach. He considered himself "a recovering psychoanalyst, *unlearning* everything my colleagues hold dear." He described this unlearning process during dream work: "The closest I can get to it is to so distance myself from what I think I know about dreams generally and this particular dream specifically so that all *a priori* assumptions are drained out of my system. Only then do I feel properly prepared to receive what is being conveyed to me from the dreamer."[14]

Beyond *a priori* assumptions

What is this draining of all assumptions? It is unlearning in its broadest sense. When there are no assumptions, there is no interpretation. Ullman expresses the above in his description of unlearning the same mental state which is found chiefly among art and religion. When all assumptions cease, when the perpetual workshop in our brains and the incessant associative clatter of thought subsides, when one's self moves out of the way of the unknown forces of creation, then, without an individual's own efforts, the inner spirit of the dream suddenly opens for a dedicated dream seeker. The invisible statue imprisoned inside the piece of rock appears as a silhouette before the eyes of a sculptor, a musician catches his melody out of the blue, a painter gives birth to his Mona Lisa, and a religious individual finds his living god beyond his own formal religion. They have *understood* something that cannot be attained through *knowledge*.

The relation between knowledge (external) and understanding (internal, experientially based knowledge, born from personal experiences) is the same as the relation between a television program and a television set. Every one of us is like a TV studio antenna, radiating both verbal and nonverbal information to surrounding areas. Our understanding is our ability to tune in to the frequency of the sender. It determines how much we are able to see from the other's broadcast. There are disturbances that can interfere with our attentiveness, like our favorite theories, into which we try to cram the transmission, blurring the image of the sender behind the snowfall static of our theoretical thinking. Our TV set may be black-and-white, unable to reproduce all the colors of another human being, causing us to see only a simplified image of the sender. We get the most out of a TV program if we submerge ourselves in it, not allowing our minds to ramble. Understanding is an immediate, direct observation, requiring stillness in order to follow the other's transmission.

Dreams are an extreme example of the type of knowledge conveyed only through direct, immediate observation, and which is easily disturbed by theoretical thinking. A lot of the information that dreams contain exists only at a "feeling level." It is easier to feel than to explain. The consequence of this is that we need sensitivity to catch everything that is radiating from the dreamer, both verbal and nonverbal, his whole being, movements, facial expressions, tone of voice, style of speech, everything.

It requires uninterrupted observation of the dreamer, the state of here-and-now, when the rambling of the listener's thoughts has calmed down as much as possible.

I thus define *understanding* very broadly. The state of understanding is an intuitive, inspirational, unrestricted receptive state. It is a state that can be sensed in the atmosphere but cannot be expressed with words. It is also often called *silent knowledge;* the concept created in the middle of the last century by scientist and philosopher Michael Polanyi. Silent knowledge, dwelling invisibly beyond *explicit knowledge,* cannot be conceptualized, unlike explicit knowledge.

Understanding is the most accurate tool of perception for observing a human mental state. Even the smartest psychological explorations and analyses cannot match up to the acuity of understanding. Learning to awaken to this state of understanding is practiced in Ullman-type dream groups.

CHAPTER FOUR

THE ESSENCE OF DREAMS

SCIENTIFIC RESEARCH

Natural sciences

Even though natural sciences and applied sciences had demonstrated their effectiveness as decoders of natural phenomena since the 17th century, they let the area of dream and sleep research wait until middle of the 20th century. Until that time there were practically no other theories about the meaning of dreams available other than Freud's psychoanalytic heritage. Ullman explained this using an allegory of a dream baby, born long ago in the womb of psychoanalysis, but still connected to the psychoanalytic afterbirth that had nurtured it in the womb, never detaching from it until the scientific experimental phase was initiated in 1953, when REM dreaming phases were discovered. This year opened the era of dream theories based on biological brain research.[15]

Chemical and electrical phenomena in the human body, including the brain, can be measured during sleep by external means. Nowadays, it can even be measured in real time with the help of computer-assisted radiology and radioactive marker substances. Chemical, electrical, and computer assisted research has yielded much information about brain physiology, among other things, that substantiate the importance of the REM dreaming phase in maintaining mental health.

Interestingly, today several areas of natural science have joined in a multidisciplinary effort to find connections between human consciousness and physical brain activity, including neurology, physiology, psychiatry, psychology, and linguistics. The increase of biological research possibilities has inspired researchers to try to build bridges between mind and body in dream areas as well. Before the modern era of cognitive neurosciences, this kind of theorizing occurred mainly among neurologists. They received most of the patients who had varieties of peculiar altered states of consciousness caused by intracranial diseases and injuries.

In spite of all these efforts and the enormous development of research instruments since the 1950s, natural sciences have not been able to yield anything to advance our knowledge of the mental nature and meaning of dreams. We need a completely different approach to find those answers.

Human sciences

Human sciences have another type of strategy. They chart traditions, customs, values, attitudes, fairytales, religions, and beliefs by means of evolution theories, psychology, cultural anthropology, and cultural history. Research of animal behavior (ethology) has cast its own sideways illumination.

Though these sciences have collected abundant dream-connected material, it remains at description-level, like the description of food, unable to convey the real taste of it. If we compare dreams with music, we can say that the natural sciences are able to disassemble a piano and cultural research can write down the opinions of the audience, but the real emotional experience can only be opened by personal, direct listening. Even an inspired account of the experience is but a faded shadow of the original one.

INTUITIVE RESEARCH

The above-mentioned empirical, classifying and analytical, high-reliability measures are able to register some external manifestations of intuitive experiences, but not the experiences themselves. As in art, even though something can indirectly be inferred from wholeness through chains of logical operations and analyses, the direct experience of wholeness is possible only through immediate personal experience. The intuitive realms of psyche, existing beyond rationality, can be contacted and revived among other means with the help of dream groups. Because there is no certain unambiguous method to understand dreams, the intuitive "I feel that... / it seems to me that..." is in all its uncertainty the "method" we must be content with, if we want to experience and understand the holistic visions of dreams.

A good example of the difference between research of experience and the experience itself is love. We can study its physical effects as accurately as ever, understanding that no investigation can illuminate its deepest essence. There is a good reason to remember the importance of being reasonable, because it's easy to forget yourself and appreciate feelings only at the expense of reason. By combining reason and intuition, we link the worlds of day and night as closely as possible without letting one of them get the upper hand, which may lead to mental imbalance.

It is, of course, advisable to investigate dream and sleeping states from many viewpoints, as is explored in this book, though its main task is to concentrate on an experiential approach. The greatest advances of science are born from collaboration of analytic knowledge and immediate intuition. This is reflected in Albert Einstein's words: "The most beautiful and profound emotion we can experience is the sensation of the mystical. It is the sower of all true science. He to whom this emotion is a stranger, who can no longer wonder and stand rapt in awe, is as good as dead."[16]

Walt Whitman declares in his poem "Song of Myself" (in *Leaves of Grass*, 1900) the same thing: "Hurrah for positive science! long live exact demonstration! [...] Gentlemen! to you the first honors always: Your facts are useful and real — and yet they are not my dwelling; (I but enter by them to an area of my dwelling.)"[17]

FREUD'S WISH FULFILLMENT

Freud began his research from the viewpoint of a natural scientist, searching first the biological base of mental states. The predecessor to his book *Interpretation of Dreams* was his manuscript, written in 1895, Project for a Scientific Psychology, where he states that "The intention [of this project] is to furnish a psychology that shall be a natural science."[18] By natural sciences, Freud meant disciplines like biology and physics that deal with matter by using measurements and experimentation. The further his research advanced, the more he realized that he had to abandon his search to find a working key for dreams in the realm of natural sciences. He created psychoanalysis instead, which developed into a self-supporting conceptual system guarding itself carefully against all external influences.

Dreams had a tremendous influence on the development of psychoanalysis. Freud stated in 1932: "The theory of dreams occupies a special place in the history of psycho-analysis and marks a turning-point; it was with it that analysis took the step from being a psychotherapeutic procedure to being a depth-psychology."[19]

Freud considered dreams to be caused by conflicts. According to him, all dreams are *wish fulfillments,* even when they do not appear to be, because then they are *disguised* fulfillments of *repressed* wishes which everyone has, but cannot allow themselves to see uncensored in broad daylight. *Dream work* suppresses these unaccepted dream thoughts by disguising them in various ways as less anxiety-provoking appearances, to the extent that their distressing content is not able to wake up the dreamer. Interpretation instead is a reverse process, aimed to open the *manifest content* in order to reveal the forbidden thoughts within. Interpretation is opposed by a *dream censor,* one of many appearances of *repression* (the most common form of defense mechanisms according to psychoanalytical thinking). In fact, during his old age Freud considered dreams to be pathological (Freud, 1932): "The dream is a pathological product, the first member of the class which includes hysterical symptoms, obsessions and delusions, but that it is distinguished from the others by its transitoriness and by its occurrence under conditions which are part of normal life."[20]

Freud's uncompromising view about every dream being wish fulfillment has aroused a great deal of discussion even in psychoanalytic literature. When a dream shows no signs of being a wish fulfillment dream, like an anxiety dream, Freud considers it a *repressed* wish, like a young boy's desire for his mother. His *desire* is disguised by the dream, letting only his *anxiety* rise to his consciousness. Regardless of the type of dream, it is possible to claim that mind is the internal battlefield of opposing systems, where the wish-provoking system is disguised, and the opposing system is visible. Freud explained in 1920 that even traumatic dreams after accidents and childhood traumas are wish fulfillments because they embody the wish to master the trauma by working it through.[21] Thus, the validation of wish fulfillment theory developed into self-supporting circular reasoning: any dream *per se* was a proof for wish fulfillment, regardless of its actual contents.

CARL GUSTAV JUNG'S HOMEOSTATIC MODEL

Almost-equally famous psychiatrist Carl Gustav Jung's (1875–1961) dream model is neither based on conflicts, nor seeing dreams as a pathological phenomenon. He considers dreams to be a self-regulating system, balancing the dreamer's one-sidedness. This dream model is *self-repairing*. Psyche as a self-regulating system maintains its equilibrium the same way the body maintains itself.

Jung, in his memoir *Memories, Dreams, Reflections*, did not see that dreams hid anything, unlike Freud: "I was never able to agree with Freud that the dream is a 'facade' behind which its meaning lies hidden a meaning already known but maliciously, so to speak, withheld from consciousness. To me dreams are a part of nature, which harbors no intention to deceive, but expresses something as best it can."[22] This is in line with Erich Fromm's view. According to Fromm there is no more censorship in dreams, except that they are expressed in the language of poetry and symbols. Dream censorship "is a 'censorship' only for people with little poetic imagination."[23]

Jung's broader view about dreams is reflected in these excerpts:

> The dream is a natural phenomenon. It does not spring from a special intention. One cannot explain it with a psychology taken from consciousness. We are dealing with a particular way of functioning independent of the human ego's will and wishes, intention or aim. It is an unintentional occurrence, just like everything occurring in nature. Therefore, we also cannot assume that the sky gets clouded only to annoy us; it simply is as it is.[24]

> So flowerlike is [the dream] in its candor and veracity that it makes us blush for the deceitfulness of our lives.[25]

> Dreams are neither deliberate nor voluntary ideas, but natural phenomena, which are anything other than what they seem

to be. They do not deceive, lie, twist or embellish but instead express naively what they are and what they mean. They irritate and mislead us only because we do not understand them.

Dreams in themselves do not want anything. They only express themselves; they are natural facts, findings like sugar in diabetic blood or typhoid fever. Only if we are wise, can we understand them as warning signs of nature. [26]

In this characterization, the words *naive* and *childlike* are essential. One of my favorite definitions of a dream is that it is *a state of innocent wisdom*. It is the most authentic dimension inside us, a childlike, innocent observation incapable of lying, as in H.C. Andersen's fairytale *The Emperor's New Clothes,* when the child sees through the false show of waking consciousness and perceives that the emperor has no clothes. When dreaming we are simply not able to lie. We are in a state where we do not know what lying is, looking at our situation in life as it really is.

FREDERICK PERLS: DREAM AS A PROJECTION OF SELF

The psychiatrist Frederick Perls (1893–1970) was an ego-centric psychopath, who from the viewpoint of civilized conduct and language belittled all other psychotherapy schools and with vulgar, egocentric style declared that we are not here to live up to each other's expectations, to satisfy each other's needs, but we are responsible only to ourselves, nobody else.[27]

From the opposite point of view, he followed his own, unique path and largely liberated himself from the power and humiliation games people play, personally living the freedom of what he taught, acutely seeing the numerous traps people set for each other trying to put everyone in the same big jumbled net of human relations. According to Perls, a therapist who tries to be helpful is doomed from the very beginning. This statement is not as harsh as it sounds. He refers to the naive response to a patient's plea, which entices the healer to support just those psychological obstacles the dreamer tries to circumvent by putting the responsibility on the healer's shoulders.

His ranting, as one-sided as it occasionally is, is refreshingly clever, especially his autobiography *In and Out the Garbage Pail* (1969), whose shameless impudence makes the reader amused more often than not. He is what he is. In all his authoritative impossibility he is more authentic than therapists who hide themselves behind their stereotypic professional roles, independent of their therapeutic orientation.

Perls' name is not as well-known as Freud's and Jung's, but the name of *Gestalt therapy*, which he developed, is more widely known, even though only a few are more familiar with the features of it. Dreams are only one sector of this therapy, but the most important one. According to Perls, dreams are the most spontaneous form of human existence. In dreams we can see our whole existence most clearly, problems and all. Every single bit of any dream is a piece of the dreamer's persona. These alienated parts of ourselves, these empty holes in our personalities, must be taken under control again and integrated back into one single entity.

The method of taking these dream parts into possession is not only *telling* the dream, but *immersing* into it by identifying successively with each living and lifeless part of the dream. In applying the *empty chair technique,* the dreamer identifies with one object or character in the dream, speaking out loud directly to another dream object which is imagined to be in the opposite, empty chair. The dreamer then changes roles and chairs, having thus a conversation with himself by moving back and forth between the two chairs.

The most significant obstacle for broader implementation of this method is its dependence on the therapist's personality. It is based on Perl's active, commanding, downright confrontational approach, which is almost impossible to adapt and apply successfully. One of his main methods is to break the client's neurotic defense by driving him into a logical blind alley. This method resembles Zen *koans* (questions without any rational answers, such as "Which tone will you get if you clap your one single hand together?"). The emphasis in this method lies more in running over than encountering the client.

MORENO'S PSYCHODRAMA

Also *psychodrama*, developed by psychiatrist Jacob Levy Moreno (1889–1974), utilizes dreams a bit like Gestalt therapy, the difference being that the dreamer does not play his dream by himself or with the leader, but as one participant in group work, where parts of the dream are dealt out as a play with changing roles to participants who impersonate them in many different combinations. *Playback Theatre,* born in the 1970s, is based on improvisation, partly resembling psychodrama. It is also suitable for enlivening both an audience's and a theatre group's own dreams.

The advantage of Gestalt therapy and psychodrama is the intentional use of body language in addition to the verbal. It heightens the odds to understand dream language, because dreams are emotional, intuitive knowledge conveyed through gestures and tone of voice more intensively than through the conceptual system of spoken language.

On the other hand, these methods disturb the understanding of dreams because the original dream is not allowed to develop by itself as untouched, as in the process Ullman has created. It is altered and modified in different ways, either intentionally as in Gestalt therapy, or unintentionally if a dream group's predefined assumptions recolor the original tone of the dream without anyone realizing it. Dreams are thereby restricted from expressing the dreamer's own inner reality as truthfully as possible, becoming instead increasingly contaminated with conscious ingredients. My own solution has been to faithfully stay with the dream, using Ullman's process as my instrument, which among all the methods I know, concentrates most accurately and extensively only on the dream. I know and I confess the value of a great many other sensitive ways to approach our nightly and daily internal images. However, I personally do not want to spend my remaining, irrevocably diminishing time on Earth with any other internal images of man than the deepest ones, most near the authentic mental core of human beings.

SOCIAL DREAMING

In 1982, Dr. Gordon Lawrence presented a socio-centric view to dreams called Social Dreaming (SD) at the Tavistock Institute of Human Relations in London. It considers dreams social in origin. SD tries to extract and purify the social contents of dreams from any dream-obscuring group dynamics containing individual egocentric orientations, which in turn would mean that the relationships of the participants would become a focus, detracting attention from the knowledge that dreams contain.

To emphasize the special nature of SD gatherings, Lawrence discarded the group concept, replacing it with a *matrix*, which is a looser structure than a group, even physically; the participants' seats are rearranged to minimize any group forming. Participants are, in a way, *alone in a group.* They form a Social Dreaming Matrix (SDM).

This loose group, this matrix, is weaving a web of feelings and thoughts, sharing the participants' dreams, associating freely from anyone's dreams, amplifying them with their own contributions: but, no one is allowed to interpret or to individualize them as belonging to any single person. SD does not wish to discover one central meaning, seeing dreams instead as elements scattering through space, creating a dynamic collage. The dream is not given a name or a definition, but is sent to float in an open, infinite space. All shared dreams create an atmosphere where individual dreams are like waves forming a social sea of dreams. SD concentrates on this sea, on dreams and not dreamers. When dreams are not attached to individuals, it is easier to see how dreams holistically reflect the general state of the whole society. SD sees the dream as belonging to the matrix and not the individual. SD thus avoids as much as possible any group dynamics, interpretations, or possibilities where the narcissism of individuals could disturb the collective image dreams are reflecting.

SD reaches for the inner, unconscious, infinite world of the psyche. Lawrence sees it as a methodology that is congruent with these unconscious processes and which does not seek refuge in conscious, unintentionally defensive reductionist ratiocination. SD succeeds in avoiding many traps of over-psychiatrization and over-pathologization of dreams.

However, by defocusing from the individual to the social sphere, in order to avoid all these disadvantages, it pays a price. It is true that it is successful in de-pathologizing dreams, and even creating an atmosphere where the contact with the infinite human soul intensifies through dreams, but the next step is where SDM for the most part loses just what it is seeking. By avoiding an individual-centered approach, it certainly has a greater chance of creating contact with the power field of infinity, but this field largely remains unfocused. Compared with Ullman groups, SDM brings forth the sunshine but does not focus it, thus creating a warm but unfocused atmosphere. An Ullman-type group works like a parabolic receiver or a magnifying glass, reflecting the energy of the sun onto one burning point who is the dreamer, who with the help of this additional energy charge is then able to drill through the surface of the waking state deeper than SDM, acting as a bridge to the unknown and as a medium amplified with the group's contribution. This concentrated, intensive energy stream may be strong enough to advance deeper, even to transpersonal dimensions. Only an individual, not a group or matrix, is able to dive into the depths beyond waking state levels. The deepest experiences are always individual ones.

SD knows that this kind of Ullman-type endeavor may remain only at an ordinary, superficial, semi-psychiatric level, but while undeniably avoiding this danger, SD loses the most poignant core of dreams. In spite of this, SD is a valuable reminder of social, common dimensions of dreams, because this fact is far too obscure in our society of worshipping the individual and his egocentricity. So, paradoxically, we cannot avoid having the individual be the focus of everyone's attention and help, in order to clearly see *beyond* the individual into social and transpersonal dimensions. When comparing SDM and the Ullman process, we could say that SDM is indefinitely infinite and the Ullman process definitely infinite. On the other hand, they both can be ruined by unenlightened people. They both are only methodological frames which are constructed to allow dreams to address our waking state as unconstrained and constructively as possible, but the real action always takes place only in human souls beyond any methodologies.

SYMBOLS, METAPHORS, MEANINGS

Dream images are often called symbols or metaphors. The boundaries between symbol, metaphor and sign are vague. Sign as unambiguous and symbol as ambiguous are opposites in the same continuum. A "STOP" traffic sign is very unambiguous, thus its nature is more sign than symbol, but despite this, it can symbolize all kinds of obstacles, refusals, and prohibitions. The symbol of the planet Venus is a symbol of woman, too, making it slightly ambiguous. The cross is much more ambiguous, pointing in the end to (the Christian) God, who, for one, is actually infinitely ambiguous; in other words, beyond any definitions.

Because one symbol can symbolize many things—otherwise, it would not be a symbol at all—no correct meaning can exist for any symbol. Correspondingly, there cannot be any correct meaning for Mona Lisa, which could be revealed by a "correct" interpretation. Even though we do not know how a certain dreamer at a certain moment uses his dream symbol, symbols are connected to the dreamer's surrounding society; therefore, symbols also have common, shareable meanings. They usually evolve gradually over generations, but they can be born at lightning speed, as in the year 2006 when Finland's heavy metal band Lord won the Eurovision song contest. An erected index finger and little finger became in one single night the status symbol for the whole Finnish nation. But what did it symbolize? The band itself or Finnish culture, heavy metal music, Satanism, evil forces or the fruits of hard, earnest work, authentic sincerity or deceptive commerciality?

The snake often symbolizes the penis. In the Bible it represents temptation and deceit, in yoga philosophy it is one of life's basic energies. Poisonous, aggressive behavior or strangling dependency on someone may be suggestive of the snake. The swastika reminds us of Nazis, but for three thousand years it has been mainly an oriental symbol for well-being, known in many countries. It was a symbol of the Finnish Air Force until World War II, still depicted on many badges of honor and on the flag of Finland's president. It is an example of a symbol containing contradictory meaning.

The only dream images which have, to some degree, relatively stable meanings, are personal symbols. When the external world, for one reason or another, actively pressures me, I easily dream military service dreams, colored by the anxiety provoked by the obligatory submission to external rules which I felt during my military service. When I absolutely must get through some difficult task because of my own, inner standards, I am sitting, in my dreams, in the most demanding examination I have experienced: the final, most important high school examination. When I was writing a description for this book about C.G. Jung's strange experiences when he was seriously ill, I dreamed of myself sitting in my high school examination where my task in a creative-writing test was to produce creative writing about Jung, and my proctor was Montague Ullman. The old professor taught me everything I know about dreams, and he was always in my mind when I was writing the Jung chapter: would Ullman accept my text? Did I dare to follow firmly only my view, or was I risking too much, losing both his and my readers' approval? Did I become disqualified in my oneirologic examination?

My other examination dream:

> *I have not read enough this year for my high school examination, so I will fail again, and year after year passing my examination will be more and more improbable because my memory has begun to falter. I am forgetting old material and new examination material will increasingly replace the old. Will it be worthwhile for an old individual to stress himself so much anymore? I start driving to the examination; I grow more and more tired, I lose consciousness and wake up at the end of a small road shrinking to a narrow path. I have lost my car.*

Three days before this dream, a medical examination revealed completely unexpectedly that I had dangerously high blood pressure. The night before the dream, I read the Finnish Medical Journal diabetes issue. I had been expecting diabetes for ten years because I had all the risk factors. Because of these incidents, my mind was filled with my own gradual physical deterioration, which had already started. Which examination of my life did I still want to pass now, at older than sixty? To get my dream book ready? The dream theme feels too insignificant in this connection. I seem to evaluate my whole life. What have I attained, what should still be attained, what must I pass before my physical and mental energies wither away? I have been very concerned about the deterioration of my memory,—familiar worries for older people—the exhaustion of my body, and my mental unconsciousness on the road of life—the time of letting go,—the time of giving up, slowing down advancement. This was the same anxiety in the dream, which once again caught the most illustrative images of anxiety from my youth, when I had to pass my most important and difficult examination that would influence my whole future.

There is a lesson in this, though, that even though your own dream symbols would feel very familiar, it is inadvisable to expect that they present the same conditions every time. There is reason to be sensitive every time to their new and multifaceted shades of meanings.

After all this talk about symbols, I must confess that I do not like the word "symbol" when talking about dreams, because the general usage of "symbol" contains a negative connotation, downgrading living dream images to a lower status, to some kind of dead, shadowlike reflections from our "more real" waking life. In spite of this I will continue to use this word, often simplistically and superficially throughout this book. It is a concession I must make because of my inability to find a better alternative. I am talking also about dream "images" and "metaphors." All three words are usually interchangeable, but they are not identical. I am not going to delve deeper into linguistic differences here, but I deal with their philosophical dimensions more in the later parts of the book.

Meaning is the invention of waking consciousness

Dream images are born in a "meaningless" state, i.e. in a state where there are no meanings. Meanings are aspects of waking consciousness. Meanings *mean* and *signify* something for our intellect. To mean something is to find an *explanation* for intellect. Meanings and explanations are *post festum*, secondary, later processes. The Mona Lisa painting does not *mean* something. Meanings are born afterwards, in retrospect in the observer's head; every observer has his unique meaning, which he projects back on the object he is observing. To give meaning to the multifaceted phenomena of dreams is easy by *pruning*; cutting off everything except those parts which seem to confirm our own pet ideas. We call this shrunken result the "meaning" of dreams.

The relationship of meaning to living contents in a dream is like the relationship of an Earth-centric worldview to a heliocentric one. We see the Sun rotating around the Earth. In accord with this perception, the Earth-centric astronomical model—despite its complexity—was able to explain the movements of planets exactly the same as the later-invented heliocentric model. The Earth-centric model was comprehensible, logical, yet fallacious. In life, as in dreams, there is more than meets the eye. A meaning given to some dream may seem very logical, explaining it nicely, but still leave the dreamer unconcerned, unmoved, untouched at the emotional level, which means that it has not yet touched the real contents of that dream. When emotional aha! reactions are aroused in the dreamer then we know that some explanation has at last begun to reflect more of the authentic contents of the dream.

The late essayist and human rights activist Susan Sontag states in her work *Against Interpretation* that interpretation violates art, making it into an article for use, squeezing it into diverse intellectual classifications, thus impoverishing it, and depleting the world in order to set up a shadow world of "meanings" instead.[28] Dreams do not have any concepts or logic, and dream symbols do not have some specific meanings of their own. The essence of dreams is reflected as meanings only when seen from a distance. Many are satisfied with this kind of viewing from far away, believing that dreams do not contain anything other than meanings, and on top of that, usually only one meaning.

To evaluate dreams with yardsticks of meanings is no more fruitful than to judge people from their shadows. When we succeed in tuning ourselves away from the shadow level of meanings towards the experiential, multidimensional visions of dreams, they rush through our whole being, creating impressionistic, truthful paintings of our life on the dream canvas. Only then are we able to see that meanings are only shadowy, frozen snapshots of ever-dancing silhouettes on the surface of our waking consciousness, originally created by the flame of life, but petrified by interpretations.

I will now wipe out even symbols for a while: dream images *per se* are not even symbols. The whole "symbol" concept and search of its "meaning" belongs to the realm of our waking consciousness, which is occupied with *post festum* activity, trying to explain in retrospect one thing with the help of another. When we dream we are up to our ears in a dream—we *are* a dream. James Hillman (1979) wrote, "At night the dream has me, but in the morning I say, I had a dream."[29] Dream *is* a reality, not any reflector of it. Dreams can begin to "mean" something only in our waking state, when we are trying to shoehorn dream's infinitude into our small bowl of intellect.[30] Dream images look deceptively like symbols, in other words *representations of something else*, only when we observe them from the narrow angle of our waking consciousness.

Like shadows, these two-dimensional creatures, are born out of their three-dimensional creators, so meanings *do* have a certain value when we try to decipher something about dreams, their creators. In the best case, meanings may be related to dreams as a view through a keyhole is related to an unrestricted view of the whole landscape. Many consider a keyhole view to be the widest view possible, because they have not yet found their path to the wider ranging landscape of dreams. Peeping through the keyhole means, however, that the first steps toward dreams have already been taken.

I cannot surpass the barriers of language. Even though I continue to speak about symbols and meanings of dreams, you must keep in mind that they are not the core material of dreams, but only the crutches our waking consciousness needs on its limping journey, searching for more powerful layers of dreams. The answers we can get when asking "what this dream means" may not be completely wrong answers, but very limited ones all the same.

When dreaming, we have stepped from the world of symbolism into the world of signalism, where nothing symbolizes something else, and where symbol interpreters are not needed anymore to cause chaos, because things are seen as what they are, as straight signals, immediately, without explanations. We do not describe and explain reality anymore, we just *are* reality.

Freud and sex

The best-known interpreter of dreams is none other than, of course, Freud. The question about sexuality in dreams cannot be avoided because of Freud's great influence; according to him the great majority of symbols are sexual by nature. He presents some of them in his Vienna 1915–1917 lectures:[31] The holy figure "3" is a symbolical substitute for male genitalia. Other male sex symbols can be those which are long and upright, such as sticks, umbrellas, poles and trees. Also, objects that have the characteristic of penetration into the body and consequent injury, hence pointed weapons of every type, knives, daggers, lances, swords, and in the same manner firearms, guns, pistols and the revolver; objects out of which water flows: faucets, water cans, fountains; objects that have the power of elongation, such as hanging lamps, etc. Snakes, fish, hats, coats, pens. Erection is symbolized by balloons, airplanes, Zeppelins and flying dreams—for women, too, because the wish to be a man is often present in women, consciously or unconsciously.

The female genitalia are symbolically represented by objects which have a space capable of being filled by something, such as pits, caves, and hollows, pitchers and bottles, boxes and trunks, jars, cases, pockets, ships, doors, churches and chapels, wood, paper, tables, books, shoes and mouth etc. Breasts as fruits, pubic hair as woods and bushes. Sweets asexual delights. Mounting ladders, ascents and steps depict sexual intercourse, likewise rhythmic activities such as dancing, riding and climbing.

Freud talks about these symbols using very self-confident expressions, like "the dreams of flying must be interpreted as erection dreams" (in women, too) and that this interpretation has been confirmed "*beyond any doubt.*" It is "*easily comprehensible*" that objects out of which water flows are penis symbols. Hats and cloaks as male sex symbols "*leave no room for doubt,*" and pencils, quills, nail files, hammers "*undoubtedly*" so, too. The cravat is an "*unmistakable*" male symbol; likewise unmistakably the snail and mussel are female ones. The most immediate interpretation of having one's teeth fall out, or having them pulled, is "*certainly*" castration as a punishment for onanism.

No wonder that such unambiguous self-confidence has been a downright invitation to attack Freud. It would be advisable to remember that this has been only one part of his dream interpretation. Freud even said later that he has never put forward the thesis that all dreams are of a sexual nature. If Freud had applied these symbols mechanically, his view would have had practically no difference from that found in any popular single-meaning dream symbol book. He knows this seeming similarity, too, warning readers in 1909: "I want to warn emphatically against overestimating the significance of symbols for dream interpretation and restricting the work of dream translation to the translating of symbols and abandoning the technique of turning the dreamer's associations to good account."[32]

Interpretation based on acquaintance with symbols is only a supplement to Freud's interpretation technique, solely unable to produce workable results. Freud listened very carefully to what the dreamer had to say, without applying blindly some standard symbol interpretation.

Sex symbols were not for Freud quite as unambiguous as he supposed.

One example of this is the bridge, which, according to him, had originally meant the male organ, which unites the two parents in sexual intercourse; but afterward it developed further meanings, which are derived from this first one, and now this symbol stands for transition or change in condition generally. Freud mentions this connection in his essay, *Revision of the Theory of Dreams*:

> Our work of interpretation uncovers, so to say, the raw material, which must often enough be described as sexual in the widest sense, but has found the most varied application in later adaptations. Derivations of this kind are apt to bring down on us the wrath of all non-analytically schooled workers, as though we were seeking to deny or undervalue everything that was later erected on the original basis.[33]

Thus, Freud on the one hand admits other meanings, yet considers the sexual meaning the *widest* meaning, which endows it a subtle *primus inter pares* (first among equals) tone.

The next dream is a good example of how careful one must be before automatically engaging oneself in a search for the dream's focus on sexuality and on the dreamer's past.

> *A woman dreamed of being at a sex fair in her childhood town. There was also the famous heavy-metal band Lordi. Plenty of people had come to see the band. A young male rocker, who belonged to the band, tried to persuade her to have sexual intercourse.*

The dreamer as a non-Christian, indifferent to religion, had promised to make a presentation on her favorite topic for Christian people in their upcoming convention. When the presentation was only one day ahead, her anxiety had risen sky-high. She knew that in connection with her presentation there would be held a Christian Mass, which heightened her anxiety still more. She had never talked to such an unfamiliar audience, whose worldview was opposite to her own. How could she talk to these people without hurting them?

She felt that her urge to speak about her favorite topic had overridden her morale. She felt she was using willingly her talent in an unworthy way for money. She was acting against her principles. Both "Mass" and "Fair" are the same word in Finnish: messu. Sex Fair = Sex Mass. Lordi = Lord = God. Lordi band = Christian group.

After a little reflection on the feelings in this dream, she had an aha! experience, becoming aware of this connection: By promising to make the presentation, she was going to *act against her principles = prostitute herself at a Christian convention = sex mass*, because of the request of *the delegate = rocker* of this *Christian group = the Lordi Band*.

One of the abstract connotations of prostituting is to act against one's principles. Our language is full of these kinds of abstract meanings, where the base meaning at the physical level contains strong emotions. Dreams can depict abstract matters only through concrete images. The original core of all our abstractions has been some concrete phenomena in the physical world, on which more and more abstract nuances and connotations have been precipitated through countless generations.

A skilled speaker and writer makes good use of the colorful palette of all the tens of thousands of words, idioms, and allegories our languages massively contain. If we compare such expressions as "I would rather not go there to entertain them" and "I will absolutely not go there to prostitute myself," we understand how much stronger dreams are able to express emotions by using an emotionally charged physical level image, but whose main weight is, in this case, notwithstanding at the abstract level. Dreams do not use correct, neutral phrases, which hide real feelings under the cover of civilized language, but—free from the attempts of conscious control to captivate them—express things as they really are, and at every level, not only at the physical one.

This dream is a representative example of how routinely digging into one's past may lead us astray. Although the dreamer was in her childhood town, the most essential fact did not point to childhood traumas but to the future: she was just going to have a presentation in that town. The emotion linked to this town was caused by the anxiety raised by her approaching future presentation, not memories of the past.

Whatever stance will be taken towards validity of Freud's view, I recommend the reader is, in this case, notwithstanding to read his dream symbol handling texts slowly and carefully, because even though dream symbol interpretations cannot routinely be applied to any dream without violating it, there is much to learn from Freud's musings about the rich variety of dreams symbols, including sexual ones. When read slowly, in depth, they open the rich imagery of the mythologies of the human mind. Accordingly, there is no need to disregard meanings, which Freud has given to the variety of symbols. However, it is essential that we do not try to push those or any other meanings, sexual or otherwise, *theoretically* to any dream, hoping that it will match, *if the dream itself does not vividly convey just the matching feeling.* Mechanical application stiffens the atmosphere, and the dreamer raises his defenses, noting if someone is sitting in the theorist's chair, throwing around interpretations taken from textbooks rather than from carefully listening to the dreamer.

As an example of one of the typical traps to interpret symbols in the sexuality-prone way of our times is one woman's *dream about a lost purse.* Like Freud says, the female genitalia are symbolically represented by all those objects which enclose a space capable of being filled by something, and a purse is one of those typical symbols which are easily interpreted as genitals and, in a somewhat broader sense, femininity. This often holds true, but only seemingly. Copied mechanically from a textbook, it is only a dead, intellectual symbol. But we can approach this purse more vividly. Let us suppose that the dreamer knows that her dream purse contained no sex-neutral objects, but exclusively only things a woman needs to emphasize her womanhood. Then this symbol begins to come to life, and we begin to feel the aura of womanhood surrounding that purse. To understand this we have not needed a single dream authority to explain to us what a purse may symbolize.

But, just as easily, this purse may represent something completely different. What if the purse did not contain any feminine items at all, but only her credit card and all her savings, and she will be economically ruined because of this accident? What if this dream purse was her mother's who was a loathsome alcoholic? Or her daughter's, who was found dead with this purse and sleeping pills lying beside her? An old/new, expensive/ cheap, ugly/fine purse? There are millions of situations where this purse— which may have thousands of different forms—may have a role. We see that there are never completely clear and unambiguous symbols that we can glue some mechanical meanings to. We must know the whole dream, all the details, before we can understand into which dimensions of the dreamer's life any dream image may point.

Jungian archetypes

Jung was for many years Freud's apprentice and advocate until a deep difference in their worldviews became so apparent that it separated them permanently. Freud considered Jung's interest in philosophies and religions as occult activities. Jung in turn felt that Freud had become entangled in his sexual theory as passionately as a true believer ever can:

> 'My dear Jung, promise me never to abandon the sexual theory. That is the most essential thing of all. You see, we must make a dogma of it, an unshakable bulwark.' He said that to me with great emotion, in the tone of a father saying, 'And promise me this one thing, my dear son: that you will go to church every Sunday!' In some astonishment I asked him, 'A bulwark against what?' To which he replied, 'Against the black tide of mud' and here he hesitated for a moment, then added 'of occultism.'[34]

Two years later, in 1912, Jung turned away from Freud and his individual level standard symbols. According to Jung, individual symbols cannot actually be given any standard meanings, and that *even sexuality itself was not the ultimate final point where interpretations could find their fulfillment, but only one of the manifestations of forces of existence, higher than all our instincts and drives.*

Even Jung had his standard symbols, and they were not individual, but collective symbols, so universal that they apply to all cultures and across all generation gaps. He called them archetypal symbols and they have a central position in his thinking. They are symbols that have no dependence on the individual and his life experiences. They appear in dreams and fairytales, mythologies, religious traditions, fantasies, confusional states, and illusions.

Archetypes are not symbols, however. They are not images, but transcendent, beyond any conscious perception, like mirrors, which do not contain any images in themselves, but are essential prerequisites as reflectors of them. They are like the "idea" of salt solution with salt crystals that have not yet begun to crystallize. The salt solution contains thus an invisible prerequisite, which does not manifest itself in the realm of perception until the crystallization process has begun. In the same way, respectively, archetypes are manifested only through archetypal symbols, which appear in forms conditioned by individual and cultural characteristics, most clearly in dreams.

The most usual Jungian archetypes are *Animus, Anima, Persona, Shadow,* and *Self.* We all have a bit of the opposite sex, too. Anima is a complementing female archetype in man, and the respective male archetype in women is Animus. Shadow archetype depicts unpleasant things in ourselves, which we have pushed aside into the shadow, away from the daylight of our consciousness. Persona is our personality, our face, our exterior towards others, like an actor's mask.

The most innate archetype is Self. It is the essence, the central core of us, which is illustrated in Jung's mandalas; usually concentric circles illustrating the limitlessness of the universe and the human soul. Closely connected with Self is *individuation;* becoming what you are. When individuation is successful, it leads to the dethroning of the conscious self from the central place in the individual's psyche. In other words, our conscious self, our ego, yields its central position as the sun, beginning to rotate in turn around the invisible Sun, which is our Self, our real individuality, our spiritual core beyond all individual experiences. Freud's ego, in turn, wants to be the King, striving for the place of Sun, because it does not recognize the existence of the other, immensely mightier Sun. Thus, to become what you are has, for Jung, a completely different, in a way even opposite, meaning. At times Jung even seems to take the view that Self is the archetype of God, or at least a link to a religious god-experience.

According to Jung, the individuation process takes place in dreams, too. When observing only single dreams, it seems that the self-regulatory mechanism of dreams does not compensate for the daily variations of mental imbalance caused by the human psyche's one-sidedness, but in longer dream series the systematical development phases of individuation—mental growth towards the real Self, which are not seen in single dream studies—become more discernible.

Jung considered this a very demanding task for a dream interpreter. He divides dreams into "little" and "big" dreams, or insignificant and significant dreams. Small, personal-level dreams function as adjustments of our one-sidedness, compensating for the disturbed balance. "Significant dreams, on the other hand, are often remembered for a lifetime, and not infrequently prove to be the richest jewel in the treasure-house of psychic experience."

Jung thought that an intelligent non-professional may well learn to interpret little dreams, but big dreams with their cross-cultural symbols can be interpreted only with a good knowledge of mythology and folklore and with an understanding of the psychology of primitive peoples and of comparative religion.

The methods used by Freud and Jung are overlapping. Both put a premium on the dreamer's associations and on the interpreter's vast knowledge of culture, especially of fairytales, myths, folklore, and religions. Freud approached these areas from the bunker of intellect and devotion to science. Jung's way was different. As a person familiar with religious experiences, he approached dreams in an experiential, subjective way. Jung's approach is not very visible in his scientific work, becoming evident only later in his autobiography *Memories, Dreams, Reflections*.

Both gentlemen classify relatively similarly the tools dream uses to present its content, but they guide the dreamer's associations differently and draw very different conclusions as to how the material should be interpreted. Freud likes a natural science approach, while Jung likes to search transcendental archetypal elements common to the whole of humankind.

Familiarity with cultures, on which both Freud and Jung laid so much stress, is a double-edged sword. The main purpose of this book is to make it easier for the dream seeker to move toward the source of immediate experience, from where the rivers of religions, myths, fairytales, and stories flow to quench the spiritual thirst of their respective societies. Familiarity with cultures may be sometimes advantageous, but it is not at all an imperative prerequisite. The source should not be mixed up with the finger pointing to it, which is why a deep knowledge of cultures can be at best only a road sign to the source, at its worst an obstacle that prevents us from seeing the object it is pointing to. Knowledge, whatever it may be, is only knowledge, not understanding. Deep cultural knowledge may entice its owner into believing that this knowledge could as such be applied to dreams. The charming beauty and vividness of flowers in the meadow can be truly appreciated only by being among them, not by studying them as flattened, lifeless collections in the herbaria or by various scientific approaches. On the other hand, one who has not yet personally been delighted by the glory of flowers may become stimulated by studying the corpses of those poor flowers to search for the living originals. This way knowledge and science may help him at least to the beginning of his journey towards dreamland.

Medard Boss: dreams do not symbolize anything

Jung considered his archetypes to be absolutely real. Medard Boss (1903–1990) was the founder of Existential Analysis. For him, Freud's and even Jung's view was too limited. Boss's way of exploring the world was phenomenological: to study and describe phenomena without any predefined assumptions, conclusions, models, theories, or generalizations in order to see the objects of study as original and authentic as possible, without any pre- or post-processing. He had claustrophobia from Freud's prison of instincts and views, which squeezed life into mere chains of cause and effect. Neither did he think highly of Jung's archetypes, considering them Jung's fantasies, constructions born from Jung's personal experiences, but which did not have much to do with reality.[35]

For Boss, dream images do not contain any disguised and censored thoughts, but imagery-rich experiential wrestling with the very same things with which we have our daily wrestling tournaments with life. According to him, there are in fact no dream symbols at all, because for him dreams do not *symbolize* anything, but are in themselves one sector of reality, to which any criteria borrowed from day consciousness cannot be applied. We do not have dreams, but they are one form of manifestations of reality in our lives, as real as waking reality. They are not referring to anything else but to themselves, and they do not contain any ready-made solutions to our problems.

When a professional career woman and her secretary, in her dream, tried to create a small garden under the railway bridge, using mirrors to bring sunlight into its darkest corners, and the small gaps between stones in the cobblestone pavement, she also continued the same fruitless daily attempt to change her dark, petrified working situation. The dream did not present any solution, but she saw her real situation more clearly in this dream. Seeing more clearly was a prerequisite for her to build her daytime solutions on a more realistic ground than before.

The world is not what we interpret it to be, but what manifests itself in the light of existence as it is. A dream is not something which we have or which we produce, but simply a part of our existence. We can easily smother this reality of existence under various interpretative layers. Thus, there is a good reason to approach the world, dreams included, without additional constructions erected by thought processes, which lead our attention away from the foundation of life. This *"attitudeless attitude"* is not possible to attain through willpower alone. It is found through understanding ripened by the general experience of life. Boss's reflections are close mental relatives to Martin Heidegger's ideas, where one of the most central ideas is *Gelassenheit*; to let things be in whatever may be their uncertainty and their mystery. It was Heidegger who was the most important teacher for Boss.

MONTAGUE ULLMAN'S DREAM VIEW

Psychiatrist and psychoanalyst Montague Ullman's dream view is nearest to that of Boss among the scholars of previous chapters. I mentioned earlier Ullman's description about draining all a *priori* assumptions from his system. It corresponds with Boss's and Heidegger's descriptions of Gelassenheit—of not tampering *here and now* with any extra speculations.

Freud and Ullman attached great importance to making good use of the dreamer's associations. The essential difference between them in this respect lies in their primary task. Freud's goal was to study the human psyche in its entirety, where dreams are but only one sector (albeit the most important one). The other differentiating factor was time—analyses tend to last for many years. Thus, the dreamer—who had patient status in Freud's studies—had ample time to let his associations meander here, there and almost everywhere.

No doubt even Ullman's goal was, like Freud's, to understand the reality and nature of the human being, even to a greater degree than

Freud, even as far as to transpersonal dimensions which Freud eschewed, but Ullman studied people almost exclusively through their dreams. Accordingly, the Ullman way to limit the dreamer's free associations was a more disciplined practice than Freud's. The dreamer's associations can be left to wander freely away from the dream only for a reasonable time, otherwise the dream begins to fade into the background, and the remaining time reserved for the process is too short.

Jung's way of utilizing associations with his *active imagination* technique is somewhere between those of Freud and Ullman. In this method the dreamer, when awake, continues his original dream, developing and testing various endings for it and coming repeatedly back again to the original dream. Ullman's method does not change the original dream at all, because every change weakens the possibility of finding the dream's own original emotional contents. Dream imagery must not be tampered with, and associations must always start from the original dream, not from images manipulated in any way.

A much cherished belief for Ullman was the role dreams play in assisting the survival of the species, possibly even *against* our own idea about what would be advantageous for us: dreams go beyond our persona that so often protects us from the full realization of the consequences of our behavior. Our dreams are truth seekers. They go by the same rules that apply to animals in the wild: the more truthful one's perception of reality, the greater the chances of survival of the individual and the species. They are a *lingua franca;* a common language of humankind, an integrating force, species unity and an incorruptible core of all human beings[36]. We are creatures driven to survive as a species by moving to an ever-expanding state of authentic interconnectedness.

Also Finnish psychologist Antti Revonsuo in his internationally well-known threat simulation theory gives to dreams a task in the survival of the human species: during the evolution of mankind threat dreams have in advance trained people to meet dangerous real-life situations more effectively, thus chances to survive have been a little better because of this preceding dream training.[37]

My spiritual father Orvo Raippamaa's idea of a spiritual leader, *spiritus rector*, the innermost, highest knowledge inside all of us, is similar to Ullman's view, albeit more extensive, including dreams as only one of the information channels from *spiritus rector* to our day consciousness: "It takes care of such things, which surpass our individual needs. It may demand actions, which are against our instinct of self-preservation. *It accepts only which is true without paying the slightest attention to if it is harmful or not for us [as individuals]*."[38]

Dreams out of therapy rooms

The dream group process Ullman developed maximizes the possibility of understanding dreams. The dream group usually consists of about 5-10 individuals studying their own dreams. The dream group process is a multi-staged group process, each session usually lasting about two to three hours, working in most instances with only one dream during this time. The dream group that follows the Ullman process is called an *Experiential Dream Group*; the group does not bring into the process outside theories and dream authorities' opinions, but the most essential material is based on the group's own, personal experiences during the group process, leading to most authentic understanding of the nature of the dream. The group puts into action Ullman's central ideas:

- Dreams indicate in metaphorical form the truths in the dreamer's life that can be brought into reach of the dreamer in his waking state.
- If we remember a dream, we are ready to encounter the information it contains.
- The effect of encounter is healing. The dreamer connects to such an area in himself that he has not previously clearly recognized. An integrative process, becoming more whole, takes place.
- Dreams can be brought to anyone's reach. The skills needed for this task can be developed.
- Even though dreams are a very personal communication made only to the dreamer, they need to be shared with more people in order to be realized most fully.

Ullman's theory differs substantially from the other theories I have described. The other authorities conceived dream work as a form of therapy; therefore professional therapists' competence and the mastering of the theoretical conceptual system of therapy orientation in question were required. Because of these requirements, these other orientations have not been able to open the dream highway for the general public, but only narrow footpaths solely for professionals. Even psychoanalysis, already with us for over one hundred years, has not been able to give any practical dream tools to the general public, but instead has made known from behind the closed therapy room doors that the competent dream work shall belong only to psychoanalysts.

Erich Fromm frets over dogmatism in his book *The Forgotten Language—An Introduction to the Understanding of Dreams, Fairy Tales, and Myths*: "[...] certain dogmatism and rigidity that has resulted from the claims of various psychoanalytic schools, each insisting that it has the only true understanding of symbolic language."

By contrast, Ullman has created a practical dream work method, which is *independent of any conceptual systems*. It does not require knowledge of any theoretical system, nor graduating degree in any doctrine or philosophy or confessional system. That's why it is possible on a large scale to take back dreams from the experts and return them to whom they rightly belong: the dreamers themselves. This is the objective for which Ullman's process has been built from the very start.

THE MANY SHAPES OF IMAGES

The fiery lava of images: the difference between Freud and Jung

Words are tailor-made for conveying the type of knowledge that can be described with concepts. It is possible to build extremely tall theoretical castles from building blocks of concepts. Additional blocks are arranged onto base blocks, trying to construct as general a theory as possible. Almost everybody knows one such construction: Euclidean plane geometry, taught in schools for decades. The base building blocks of this concept system are called axioms (the most widely known is that two parallel lines never meet, no matter how far they are extended). The castle of the whole plane geometry system was thus built by combining these base blocks with each other.

Freud built his system in this way, advancing from observational details towards a more and more general psychoanalytic theory. He tried to see the wholeness with the help of combinations of details, piecing them together to give rise to a higher system. His construction can be compared to the Tower of Babel, which was built more for the praise of man's intellect than for forces beyond.

Jung's theory was born in an opposite, top-down method, from the more general to the more specific, contrary to Freud's bottom-up approach. Jung was plunged into a very intensive flood of images, for which he then searched appropriate expressions for decades. These image-intensive experiences began when he was 37 years old. He let himself fall into an intensive inner vision, which launched a four-year long deluge of visions:

> But then, I hit upon this stream of lava, and the heat of its fires reshaped my life. That was the primal stuff which compelled me to work upon it, and my works are a more or less successful endeavor to incorporate this incandescent matter into the contemporary picture of the world—the later details are only supplements and clarifications of the material that burst forth from the unconscious, and at first swamped me. It was the prima materia for a lifetime's work.

> Today [at 87 years old] I can say that I have never lost touch with my initial experiences. All my works, all my creative activity, has come from those initial fantasies and dreams, which began in 1912, almost fifty years ago. Everything that I accomplished in later life was already contained in them, although at first only in the form of emotions and images.

Images, experienced in both his nightly dreams and his daytime fantasies, were the fiery lava from which his conceptual rock of scientific work was crystallized.

Regarding dream exploration, Jung's starting point was more fruitful than Freud's, because Jung's material gushed out spontaneously and vividly from same internal sources, where also dreams rise to the surface of waking consciousness. Freud, unable to perceive the inner visions spontaneously, had to approach dreams from the angle of scientific analysis, and was compelled to erect his analytical construction with his own work.

Freud found only that which was possible for him to find—this utterance, which sounds to be a mere circular reasoning, is of course valid for every human being on Earth. He had only three of life's four dimensions in his own consciousness and in his theory of dreams. The *individual* dimension was the primary one, after that came the *biological*, and later in his life, increasingly, the social dimension. However, what Freud was lacking was the *fourth* dimension, which has no specific name but can be called transpersonal, cosmic, transcendental, etc. This lack made it possible for him to leave psyche in the animal-like state, where primarily lower drives and instincts reign and rage. Jung characterized:

> [M]any dreams present images and associations that are analogous to primitive ideas, myths, and rites. These dream images were called "archaic remnants" by Freud; the phrase suggests that they are psychic elements surviving in the human mind from ages long ago. This point of view is characteristic of those who regard the unconscious as a mere appendix of consciousness (or, more picturesquely, as a trash can that collects all the refuse of the conscious mind).[39]

It is especially interesting how Freud deals with this deficiency, because it illuminates to us the very human characteristic of believing reality to be congruent with one's sense impressions. The great majority of humankind commits the same mistake. What makes this especially interesting is the fact that Freud, who with his accurate observations found inside his own psyche the world hidden from our waking consciousness, follows the majority in this respect.

Freud ignored experiences beyond his world view and personal experience, explaining them to be religiously colored fantasies and primitive remnants from early babyhood experiences. The rigidness of his negative attitude manifests itself in a conviction expressed in later life: "I am firmly convinced that the most careful elaboration of the material upon which the problems of religion are based would not shake these conclusions [of psychoanalysis, for ex.: 'religion … as a parallel to the neurosis which the civilized individual must pass through on his way from childhood to maturity']."[40]

The opposite approach to Freud's solution is to put one's own intellect aside and give oneself up to blind good-hearted trust without any personal transcendental experiences.

A third major way is along Heidegger's lines in *Gelassenheit,* to let things just be without any extra attitudes and mental constructions attached to them. The sign of this *"attitudeless attitude"* is to know one's own ignorance. It is also an essential aspect of dream groups, where one, after seeing repeatedly how easy it is to make mistakes in one's evaluations of a fellowman, may begin to understand how little we understand, and begin to listen, to hear, without any deafening preconceived ideas.

Let us compare the massive certainty of Freud's statements with the "Retrospect" chapter of Jung's memoirs: "I cannot form any final judgment because the phenomenon of man is too vast. The older I have become, the less I have understood or had insight into or known about myself. […] I have no judgment about myself and my life. There is nothing I am quite sure about. I have no definite convictions—not about anything, really."[41]

Thus Freud's work, as clearly as it does verify the magnificent sharpness of his thinking, does not reach as far to the wholeness of the human being as Jung's accomplishments. However, it is Freud's life work which has become more widely known, being more understandable in our culture, which has become estranged from transpersonal dimensions and has moved in the direction of intellect, analysis and science. Jung's view has not managed to strike as strongly the right chord in our society's consciousness.

Compared to Jung's view, Freud saw the human being as a considerably more limited creature, thus he had no difficulty in believing in his own intellectual capacity and acuteness of perception. He felt himself entitled to say, "Our best hope for the future is that the intellect— the scientific spirit,—reason—should in time establish a dictatorship over the human mind." It's no wonder that he ventured to give to symbols such strong constant meanings, that they acquired the status of almost absolute truths in his mind.

Images of language

Similar experiences of images, such as Jung's lava stream described in the previous chapter, are happening to almost all of us, but in a less vigorous way. Dreams are direct channels for the pictures of the soul to rise to the waking consciousness, but they stream to our conscious domain through more indirect channels as well, as all kinds of pictures, through physical paintings, performing arts, and metaphors of language, especially poetry.

Poetry is the form of language that is able to set our inner images to fire the most intensely. The poet Jim Harrison writes: "As a poet I am the bird, not the ornithologist."[42] The most magnificent, unbelievably brilliant conjurer of Finnish language images is the writer Volter Kilpi (1874–1939). His series of books, written 1933-1937, telling of the inhabitants of the Turku archipelago in Finland, contain the energy of the finest poetry. He described how the innermost images of his soul flared up, shaping themselves into words, which move their audience as forcefully as dreams: "Only from within our own self, without any hesitation, without any doubt, from sentiments superheated into flaming red words, must those words be allowed to blaze out. Only then their golden truth is dazzling brightly."[43, 44, 45, 46]

Almost every human being, when speaking, is using forms of metaphor and allegory. Usually we do not take note of the lingual, pictorial effects we are using, and still less we consume our time by pondering from which sources those images have originated. The metaphors of our everyday language differ from our nightly images by not containing personal emotional condensations, but instead are so diluted in general use, that their literal meaning flashes to our minds only infrequently. For example, we may say quite automatically that a rolling stone gathers no moss and warn about putting all our eggs in one basket without ever thinking about the origins of those phrases, or even the original meaning.

Dreams seem to be capable of using the multifaceted meanings of many words as puns and double entendres. The diversity of these meanings has been connected with their images already before we go to sleep. When dreaming we are able to utilize the rich palette of meanings and are thus able to illustrate even abstract matters with the help of physical images. A lively speaking person is able to paint with words, able to revive old linguistic images flattened by general usage. One picture is worth a thousand words in the daytime, too, but only dreams are the real wizards of resurrecting images.

I suppose that only very few have created a mental picture of language as "a tongue," but this physical meaning is still found in the expression "mother tongue." This is but one example among innumerable others of how the abstract meaning is also attached to a physical object in our daytime mother tongue. A physical object symbolizing another one is, for example, the tongue on a shoe, and so on. A figurative expression of an abstract meaning at the concrete level is the tongue image in the next dream:

> *The dreamer's tongue breaks into pieces in her mouth and efforts to spit it out cause her mouth to foam bubbles, which have changed into pearls. However the pearl surfaces have been wiped away, revealing their bloody contents.*

The dreamer felt that she had talked too much about her work within creative arts. She was *foaming at the mouth*, trying with her own *tongue* and with *pearls of wisdom* to convince her stubborn listeners, but had not succeeded in her endeavor. This caused her to distrust herself, the value of her creativeness, feeling her language disintegrate, the pearls of her words' bloody wounded surface revealed.

I heard a fascinating example of the multidimensionality of words when participating in a Nordic and European Network dream conference outside London. During my demo session, one of the participants had dreamed that the big Ferris wheel in London, the London Eye, was going to crash down into the River Thames. When the group suggested the double meaning of "Eye" and "I" because they are pronounced similarly, the dreamer immediately saw a connection. He felt that his London "I," his ego, was about to fall apart. He was afraid of returning to London where human relationship problems were waiting for him, threatening to bring down his self-image.

A dream does not need to make an exact copy of the outward situation that originally launched the dream image, but instead it can wrap the associated feeling inside the combinations of images borrowed from earlier experiences where the dreamer has had the same feeling. These images can have their origin both in individual as well as collective experiences received already from the dreamer's earliest infancy. These collective images may have especially concentrated emotional connotations, crystallized through many generations, expressing themselves in numerous common expressions and proverbs.

The red thread of feelings

When I heard that my publisher would make a publishing contract with me concerning this dream book, I tossed and turned restlessly in my bed the next night. At half past three in the morning I decided to go to my computer and at last begin to write my book to release the pressure that had accumulated inside me. On standing up I suddenly had a mental image of *a bear who shoots a resin bung from its behind when waking up from his winter sleep.* Not a very poetic beginning for my book! My own view of dreams had, during its hibernation, waited for an external helper to remove that bung, to release my writer's block. Where did this image come from? I'm still not sure to this day.

Emotional waves, which for one reason or another have not calmed down during the day, continue to await resolution by expressing themselves as dreams, as moving images for one and one half hours every night. Our memory banks open to unparalleled depths over time and space, and a parade of people, animals, places, landscapes, events, and the long deceased march out waving flags of the same unresolved emotions that we have in our present life situation.

Frequently, we or other people in our dreams area different age than in reality. In those cases, it is worthwhile to examine carefully what has happened at the time to which the dream age points. A mother was frightened by her dream in which her son died. In reality her son was alive and already a teenager, while in the dream he was only four years old. She realized that he had been in danger then, as much danger as he was when the dream occurred, in the present time. She recognized that her fear was the same in both cases. The same emotion was the common factor linking these two ages and incidents together.

The stars in the sunshine

The dream-producing emotional layers of our psyche do not vanish anywhere during the day, just like stars are still in place, albeit invisible, when the bright sun of the day draws all our attention. For the majority of people, it is not easy to perceive every emotion, even intensive ones, flashing swiftly into the consciousness and vanishing from sight again. We may repress them actively, or we are too occupied with our daily routines, or we are simply too inexperienced with introspection.

The most well-known test which reveals emotions moving under our waking consciousness is Rorschach's inkblot test onto whose blots the mental images of the person being tested are superimposed. When a mortally ill person walking in the park begins to see the crossing branches of trees as gravestone crosses, it is easy to understand that he projects his mental images to the external world, his fears coloring and shaping his perceptions, whereas it is much more difficult to become aware how completely these inner images dominate in *each and every* observation we have, even when we assume that we are viewing the world objectively. Our life is full of these kinds of hints pointing to the extreme subjectivity of our reality. The ecstasy of falling in love, the agony of divorce, how differently we see the whole world in these two emotional states! Despite these facts we are almost always unable to draw the ultimate conclusions about the extreme subjectivity of our observations and about the serious limitations to our perceptual capacity.

The most abundant mental images are our memories, otherwise we would be unable to find the way even to our local grocery store. Once when I was walking in the park near my home, a jackdaw bird passed by me on immobile wings, gliding silently in the air. A small model glider I had owned in my childhood flashed immediately in my mind. This image was neutral, gliding silently, slung into air from the child's hand. But wait! It was not a neutral image—I recalled immediately the child's happiness with his small glider, which he had, for a fleeting moment, freed from the grip of gravity, and his burning desire to be able to fly himself, to be free, to overcome the heaviness of life, if even for this passing, fleeting moment. The same burning longing for freedom now flickered inside me again as I continued my walk in the park with heavy steps and heavy thoughts. There it was again; the dreamlike connective feeling linking up the child with his glider and the old man with the bird, wiping out the decades between them as if time did not exist at all in this magical bitter-sweet moment.

The significance of feelings we have experienced in the daytime but left unnoticed is clearly revealed when studying dreams, especially when searching for the emotional context of the dream by going carefully through the previous day's activities. It is often possible to discover that the day has contained highly charged situations, but whose emotional components have been flushed away from the consciousness into the depths of our minds, from where they surge back in our next night dreams. Through the discovery of these emotional connections between day and night we can more clearly see the common roots of both day and night images.

> *I dreamed about the train that was rushing along inside a bigger train. The train, driven by an unknown driver, banged open the doors between compartments with extreme skill so that nobody was hurt, though often the collision was close. I wondered and admired the skillful, unknown train driver who was somewhere at the other end of the train.*

Usually I do not understand the connections between my dreams and the preceding day. This time however I had an aha! experience. I remembered my almost manic, extremely efficient and intuitive activity at my job, especially two successful encounters. I had steamed through that day at such a pace that it struck me that I steamed forward like a train, and that I had been a bit frightened of colliding with people I met on that particular day, but all went well. My self-centered need to keep all the glory of that day to myself kept bothering me, because the honor belonged to that unknown train driver beyond my conscious ego, not to me. The whole day, all my activities were in his hands, not mine. My old train poem with a theme of people travelling through their life in the hands of the eternally unknown train driver recurred to me. My emotional rush had not calmed down in the course of that day, and so having the same emotional state during sleep, I again traveled that night in my train, whose symbolism was already near and familiar to me.

In dreams our conscious mind cannot disturb, dim and twist our real feelings about our real state of affairs. Our cerebral cortex, able to manipulate, intrigue and invent excuses, has been shut down by our nightly dream switch. Then we are in a childlike state of innocence where we see what we really are. Unfortunately, when we wake up next morning we cannot usually understand our nightly theater—written, directed, and played by us in our own stage setting and seen by us as the only audience—because the language of the play has been so strange, so incomprehensible. We try to find in it the language we have been accustomed to in the daytime, usually without success, remaining perplexed, because we try to see it from the view of daytime, from the same fruitless, narrow standpoint, which is one of the things that caused the dream in the first place. Because of this, trying to understand our own dreams without any additional views from others is usually troublesome. Also, in my previous train dream example there are many details I could not understand. I would have understood it perhaps better if I had shared it with others in a dream group.

The criteria for understanding dreams; the aha! moment

Should I find sexuality in this train dream of mine? Trains; a classic penis symbol, seem to be so very apparent in it. My train is plowing forward, slamming the vaginal compartment doors open, penetrating the compartment, continuing its way through the next compartments? Train symbolism seems to fit well into the fact that a man cannot rid himself of his hormones, that the penetrating power of sexuality is torturing men throughout the ages and across cultures. Every alternative, including these, must be taken into consideration when we are reflecting upon a dream.

There is only one catch in this explanation. It did not touch me at all on the emotional level. It simply did not seem to fit.

Another example:

> I dreamed about a gun. I shot carelessly towards an unknown house. The bullet, flying obliquely upwards, penetrated the house, making a big hole in the roof. Nobody was hurt, but I was worried about the roof, because it will rain into the house and on the unknown people there inside.

Only mechanical symbols occurred to my mind: house = ego. Gun = penis. Bullet obliquely upwards = erection and ejaculation. But again: my feeling did not verify this.

However, if I thought about the dream along Freudian lines, I might consider the possibility that I had in the first dream repressed my sexuality and then sublimated it (transformed my sexual desire into socially useful achievements). And yet if I choose to study it from a Jungian perspective, I could draw the conclusion that perhaps the power which motivated me during the day before the dream did not originate from my drives or instincts, but from some greater power of existence, which did not appear through the sexual channel but created a completely different type of force field. Thus sexuality did not necessarily need to have either hidden or visible connections with my daytime activities and the next night's dream.

The problem is same in the second dream. When reflecting on it, I recognized a sense of general guilt because throughout my life, I have been too afraid of doing something harmful to other people. And then I shoot towards a house, carelessly, regretting what I have done. These reflect more on my basic way to communicate with the world. Sex is but a small factor in this.

We all have feelings following us through our lives, like thorns in the flesh, signaling the *ontological obstacles* which one can never win and surpass and leave behind, and which not even therapies, dreams, religions, or snake oil can cure. Those feelings are like spice in the soup, always adding its own hue whatever you drink and eat. It colors more or less everything. These feelings are like *borduna* in music, a basic note or chord continuing in the background throughout the symphony of life, establishing the basic tonality upon which the life is colored. These feelings vary from day to day, caused by different events, but there they always are, in religious parlance, our own portion of the original sin of humankind echoing from the depths of human souls and also through dreams.

What are the criteria, then, that I apply when evaluating the dream contents? Understanding dreams is not an intellectual construction, especially not the kind of construction whose sole purpose is to capture and massage dream images for so long that they can fit nicely into some background theory. Our intellect is very ingenious, capable of explaining and cramming any and every phenomena into the pet bag of our favorite theory, as we very well see around us when observing myriad religious and political orientations. In spite of the fact that we are observing the very same world, we draw even completely opposite conclusions of what we think we have seen. There is some crucial factor in us, separating us from each other, something which twists and impoverishes our observations, casting us into the prison cells of our differing opinions, and from which so very few seem to find their way out again.

Interpreting dreams is explaining dreams. Explaining is serving something beyond our grasp in such a pre-digested form that our intellect is able to cope with it. Intellect coping with something is knowledge, but it is not at all sure if this knowledge is right or wrong, or if it has anything to do with the original phenomena. We may have extreme amounts of knowledge about people without necessarily being able to understand them at all. It is very characteristic for our culture to identify reality with the ability to explain it: if the knowledge is not *evidence-based* knowledge, it is supposed to be false, incorrect knowledge. This same requirement is often applied to dreams. Our waking consciousness loves to seek out as unambiguous meanings for dreams as possible. This attitude is essential for scientific approaches, but applied to dreams, it mutilates them, chopping them into lifeless pieces, pruning and clipping off a bit here and another bit there, taking shortcuts, simplifying the dreams in order to fit them inside the Procrustean bed.

The danger signals indicating that a dream is being mutilated are expressions which convey that a final decision, a final statement about the meaning of a dream, have been made. The most typical of these expressions are *"as a matter of fact"* and *"actually."* They point to a blind alley, to a seemingly final outcome, where the *true* meaning of a dream is imagined to be revealed. The more useful criterion of understanding dreams is *the aha! moment*. It is not a thought, but a vision, a high-speed emotional impact. It is not a product of cool, rational thinking consisting of a chain of logical operations, but an overall emotional experience, like a dream itself.

It is also a physical experience, as emotions generally are. Many dreamers have described these bodily reactions as a shiver, a chill, goose bumps, face flushing, heart pounding; we have experienced all these reactions so many times during our lives and we know they are associated with feelings. The language of feelings is the language of dreams. When the living contents of a dream are at last hatching out of the eggshell of intellect and logic into the conscious world, it is an immediate experience that does not need any interpretation mechanisms to be understood. The dream flower bursting into blossom is so clearly visible that there is no need to explain it, and no explanations could convey its blazing, multifarious colors.

Especially from a scientific standpoint, an aha! experience is a very weak criterion to prove that something real has been found. It may mean that this conclusion has been drawn only on the grounds of *emotional reasoning*, from outside sentiments projected onto the dream, which are not balanced with critical thinking. An emotional insight does not by any means exclude intellect, which is a peerless aid in putting the attained insights to use in our daily living. It is a question of balance: when intelligence is subordinated to emotions, it leads to indiscriminate emotional reasoning, and when emotions are subordinated to intellect, it leads to spiritless *as-a-matter-of-fact* theories.

Images of individual and society

Once when listening to two women discussing their breast cancers, I suddenly saw *a frozen lake with two holes in the ice*. This lake image was one of those countless images flashing into our minds over the course of the day, especially when our minds are in a non-attentive state, like just before falling to sleep or when listening to a boring lecture.

What was the connecting element between the lake and breast cancer? This daytime image was as mysterious at first as most dream images are. This time, however, I managed to find the connection. When listening to these two ladies, I was deeply wrapped up in my thoughts about the general nature of cancers. I consider the spreading of cancerous tumors more as a systemic, non-local disease; in other words as a general weakness of our whole biological system, and not so much as a local system illness which spreads with the help of seeding cancer cells to new places in an otherwise healthy biological system. Therefore, even if the local tumors could be removed, we still have the same predisposition to new tumors, i.e., we still walk on thin ice, and at any moment we may fall through and be sucked down, and another tumor may appear. This image, surfaced from beyond my consciousness, illustrated very accurately my thoughts, helping me to recognize my emotional tension.

This image appeared to me in a waking state. It might well have appeared to me in the next night's dream if I had not seen it in the daytime, thus helping to discharge the emotional component of it. The connection between the image and the objective reason for that image (i.e. cancer discussion) had been practically unreachable by logic, because they did not have any recognizable common visible components, whereas the emotional connection was crystal clear. This connection was hidden only for the intellect, not for the emotions.

This image is one example of how we are able to help dreamers to understand their own dreams, even though we do not know anything about the experiences that caused them. We are swimming in the same social sea, where our individual modifications of collective images go back to the vast reservoir of our common social imagery, which reflects our collective experiences as a society. Our own individual images are always rooted in this common social imagery. Because of this we may help the dreamer with our own images, even if we do not know him. Compared with the moving, living images of dreams, our spoken language is, of course, much more inaccurate, but it is often enough to help the dreamer find his way more and more towards the dynamic contents of his dream. We also receive many nonverbal clues from the dreamer, and these have a contributory influence on our efforts to help him.

If I had shared my lake image with the group, someone would have probably quickly found from our culture's general reservoir a common cultural image closely resembling my own image, namely the abstract, emotional *collective* meaning of being on thin ice—*to be in a dangerous situation*—which is a common expression used to describe situations where the danger is not yet visible, but imminent. He would have understood that I had felt the danger, but he would not have known at all from which *personal* situation this image had originated. Collective cultural images are able only partly to illustrate individual emotional currents. Only the owner of the image, in this case, me, could connect it to the anxiety which this cancer discussion had aroused in me. Others can function as midwives for a dream, but only the dreamer (or the receiver of a mental image in a waking state) is able to give birth to a dream baby.

The cultural part is very obvious in this example, because for inhabitants in warmer latitudes it is harder to understand how strong the collective symbol of walking on thin ice can be for a nation of thousands of lakes, such as Finland, where many have lost their loved ones through treacherously thin ice. Without this kind of collective imagery, we are more helpless to understand each other and each other's dreams. Dream imagery is the most universal language, *lingua franca,* for all of humankind, reaching over all cultures and ages.

Dreams as reflectors of the inner and outer world

It is relatively common to suppose that every part of a dream symbolizes the "I"; "me", the ego, the Self. One dreamer had come to a dream group only because her employer ordered her to do so. No wonder she had an indifferent, nonchalant attitude toward dreams. Anyway, she told her own dream. I still remember vividly how this person suddenly flinched when she realized that in her dream the person with whom she had a passionate argument was herself. The other side of her knew better than she what was not right in her life, and now she suddenly heard what her psyche wanted to say. The power of the dream image made her understand how the human psyche is richer than she had previously believed.

Another example of the discovery of the ego in an unexpected place was the dream "*How to kill the grandma*":

> *A woman in a senior position at her workplace dreamed that, together with her two brothers, she was carrying her old mother to the edge of a cliff, from where that useless old woman was supposed to be thrown down into the abyss, away from the younger generation.*

The dreamer was astonished. She really did not want to be in this gang to kill her old mother, who in reality had been dead for several years already, nor did she have any younger brothers. The feeling of the dream was very distressing. She shared this dream in a dream group, which worked with it over an hour before she recognized the old woman: it was herself! She also recognized her brothers when she realized that the feeling of the dream was the same as at her workplace: because of an organizational change, power-seeking, cocky young male colleagues wanted to eliminate her from her position. A colleague is often called a *brother* in Finnish. These were her two younger dream brothers! Just as in her dream, in reality she was helping to kill herself by complying with the organizational changes, although she still felt that she was needed at work. The dream depicted clearly those younger aspirants to power, but also her own basic attitude toward those pretenders. She preferred to step aside rather than put up a fight. She even helped to carry herself to the edge of the cliff.

When familiar objects like houses, people, whatever, in a dream seem to be different from their real counterparts, it is a sign that the dream is telling about something else than it originally appears to be. Our tendency to try to find simple, clear, unambiguous answers often leads to dismissing these differences between reality and dream images. In dream groups, this need to ignore details by simplifying is often seen when the dreamer initially describes the dream, mentioning alterations from reality (such as different hair color or style), but no one takes note. Often, the dreamer does not even notice these differences if not specifically asked about them. *Everything* in any dream should be taken into consideration. Quite often the dream person turns out to be a combination of two or more persons; one of them may even be the *dreamer*. These dream persons may show character traits which are visible but unnoticed in their waking lives, but our own prejudices and our own character traits are also projected onto them.

This leads to seemingly unsolved question about how much those dream persons are built from their "real" selves and how much from our own subjective projections. Both views have their supporters. As a matter of fact, *the real problem does not lie in the dream at all*, but in our way of perceiving our *daytime* world where we, deceived by our senses, suppose the observer is separated from the observed; i.e., we think that what we experience in the daytime, is objective.

CHAPTER FIVE

METHODS FOR UNDERSTANDING DREAMS

ROUTINE, EXPERTISE, VIRTUOSITY

The title of this chapter is paradoxical, because there are no *methods* or *techniques* which could lead to understanding. These two words bring to mind something which is *repeatedly*, *automatically*, *routinely* done. They have a slight flavor of trick, stunt, gimmick, some rehearsed *procedure*, which is easily, swiftly done, like a magic trick which only an *expert* is able to master. There is something very *constant* in all this. The routine is a *standardized*, *mechanical* course of action. All these words reflect the danger of losing playfulness, curiosity, freshness, novelty, innovation, the desire for exploration for new experiences, discoveries, the intuitive approach to the world, including the uniqueness of dreams.

Totally mastering a routine is often called *expertise,* and, at the highest level, even *virtuosity.* We all know, for example, virtuous speakers, especially among religious and political leaders, who seem to be able to explain practically any phenomena with the help of their own concept systems and theories. But in the long run even the highest virtuosity loses its mesmerizing power if it lacks genuineness, authenticity, and vivacity; in other words, *the continuity of uniqueness*, non–repeatability, the essence of life.

There are two types of virtuosity. *Technical virtuosity* is at its best very fascinating, but only for a limited time. For example, the totally perfect, aesthetic shapes dancing on the computer monitor may be enchantingly beautiful. But all this is happening inside firmly defined *limitations*, be it mathematical equations metamorphosing into a perfect dance of aesthetical curves on the computer screen or any other skillful but spiritless human performance. Nothing more is needed in many areas of life, and we need massive amounts of repetition, similarity, standardization and foreseeable reliability in order to cope with our ever-changing world.

In the world of dream interpretation, there are many who do not want anything more than someone having technical virtuosity. An intelligently worded dream interpretation may enchant listeners so thoroughly that they find in the interpreter a new leader, a new dream guru, who they begin to follow, thus straying from the path of genuine authenticity. This process is one form of finding The Right One, of being saved to some religion, to some political party, or to whatever belief system, which eagerly offers its own interpretations about what is right and what is wrong in this world.

More extensive than technical virtuosity is *virtuosity of life,* or being *a connoisseur of the art of living.* At best it has no limitations, because it is receiving the *limitlessness* of life as it is. There have always been great teachers of life who have taught their students to meet the world directly. They have taught to be independent from any teachings, *even from their own.* Quite a paradox if viewed from the standpoint of intellect alone. "Become independent from any methods with the help of my method!" I remember one incident forty years ago, when I visited one small mystic sect, where every member of this sect had the same firm opinion that, of course, it is allowed and even recommended for people to have different opinions. When I uttered my different opinion about this, I became instantaneously *persona non grata.*

Learning to understand dreams is to learn to understand life itself. It is learning through dreams, not through dream interpreters. How can we find the most fruitful way to understanding dreams through our own means without sacrificing our dreams on the interpretative altar of some dream authority? We cannot rid ourselves completely from each other's influences, and we have to take the risk of losing our own way because we need help from others in our endeavor to understand dreams and life. We are children of our culture, but at the same time its prisoners, unable to cast everything aside that we have learned, unable to invent all wheels again. How do we learn from each other without being imprisoned in the process? How do we find the one and only, lone way of our unique essence, a way which cannot be found by others on our behalf, where no one can walk but us, alone?

UNDERSTANDING DREAMS ON ONE'S OWN

Most readers would like to learn how to understand one's own dreams by oneself, independently from others. It is possible, but only to a limited extent. Dreams are more easily opened with the help of another person, but most easily in the small group of five to ten persons. I will go through all these three circumstances. They contain many common elements, which is why I have to repeat the most important principles in each of them.

Remembering dreams

Remembering dreams is of course the first condition in trying to understand them. Some people say that they do not dream. Everybody dreams, about three to five times per night, adding up to one and a half hours per night, regardless of whether one remembers them or not. If a dreamer is aroused from sleep when his eyes move under his eyelids, then almost all remember some excerpts from their dream, because we dream during the so called REM-phase, which has been named after this moving of eyes: REM stands for Rapid Eye Movement.

The fluctuation in remembering dreams is familiar to almost everyone. Days, weeks, or even months may pass by without any remembrance of dreams, then it may be followed by an intense dreaming phase of many days or weeks. Every now and then the amount of remembering may be clearly connected to changes in the dreamer's life situation.

The most prominent factor which heightens the amount of dreams remembered is *motivation*. The more one becomes interested in remembering dreams, the more one becomes motivated to trouble oneself with the extra work of trying to catch them on paper or on a tape recorder, and the more one learns to avoid the most typical error of jumping immediately out of bed to the bathroom. We all know how swiftly dreams begin to evaporate from memory on the way there. Even a change of position in bed immediately after awakening is enough to eradicate the dream.

When this preliminary work has been done and the dream has been saved in the memory, but preferably on paper, the actual work is about to begin.

Searching the recent emotional context

Previous day

Saving only the dream is still relatively inefficient. In addition to jotting down the dream, it is worthwhile to write down *the events of the previous day* in order to find all the emotion-filled moments which may have helped generate the dream. What happened on that particular day, what did you do, think and, above all, what did you feel? It is recommended to go through the whole day *slowly*, trying to recall every moment you had some feelings in the day.

"I was at work, went shopping, drove the children home from school, my mother called, I watched TV, went to bed—nothing special on that day."—No, it does not work so fast. You have to dive *deeply* into the previous day, to give it time to flow and swell back to your memory, with all the emotions. Then it may be possible to note even those emotion-filled moments which flashed and disappeared swiftly, unnoticed, because there was so many other things drawing your attention away from these feeling, or, alternatively, the feeling were so painful, that you actively pushed them away from your mind. Sometimes you may find those painful moments relatively easy:

> My mother called—communication between mother and her adult daughter are seldom completely neutral. What were we discussing during that telephone call?—Oh my goodness—my mother tried to step into my life again with her rules, orders, instructions, and directions, and I trembled with rage, unable to express it to my mother. Even

my husband has never defended me in these situations, just like yesterday when he said again: "stop that whining, will you?"—And this feeling... yes, it really is the same feeling I had in my dream about being closed in a prison cell, keys thrown away, nobody hearing my anguish.

You need ample time to recollect the memories of the previous day of the dream, and the more time that has passed, the longer you need. Thus a careful, thorough, unhurried recollection of the previous day, hour by hour, may lead to the causes of the dream. It is essential to find the specific problematic moments that triggered such emotional tensions and could not be solved during the same day, thus remaining active, producing dreams during the next night.

The most often unused clue to the dream is remembering the dream unexpectedly in the middle of the *following* day, perhaps even many days later. It never occurs by chance, but the situation in which the dream is remembered has something in common with the dream's dynamic content, and is thus an important key to it. Thus you should immediately stop and pay attention to what is happening exactly at that moment when the dream recall takes place. What did you see, hear, feel, and think?

Dream diary

If you are interested enough to keep a dream diary, do not forget to write down all the possible connections between the dream and waking life. If you write down only dreams, they remain isolated and incomprehensible in their own sphere without any connections to your waking life. Writing down events of the previous day and searching actively for connecting elements between them makes your diary an interesting story of your whole life, an autobiography which illuminates your life at a much deeper level, preserving the value of your diary even for future generations.

Freud had a cynical attitude towards dream diaries. According to him, writing down the dream deprives the repression mechanism the opportunity to forget the dream. Thus the resistance against remembering it must find another channel, which leads the repression mechanism to block the dream associations instead of forgetting the dream altogether.

Despite this rather pessimistic attitude, there is no reason *not* to write down dreams. To begin with, if the dream is remembered, it is ready for scrutinizing, albeit usually with great difficulty. Besides, we do not forget dreams only because of our resistance, but simply because dreams are being forgotten just like any other matter. There are few who remember practically everything all the time. Who could always remember all the things we should buy in a grocery store? Forgetting to buy eggs does not have to mean that some resistive mental forces are actively operative. Thus writing down pays off.

The third factor affecting the accurate dream recall is our need to understand things logically and unambiguously. We may inadvertently and unconsciously change the most obscure parts by adding, taking away, or replacing them with more clear material in order to make the images and storyline more comprehensible. The tendency of forgetting dreams can be seen in dreams groups if the dreamer first tells the dream without written notes, and then with. Only a few hours have been enough time to drop or distort relatively large chunks of the dream in the dreamer's memory. Every transformed and forgotten part means diminished chances of understanding the dream. Therefore, written notes are warmly recommended, not only when working alone, but especially if the dream is to be shared in a group.

The fishing question

After the previous day has been inspected, it is necessary to cast a glance further back into the past, often from a few days to a few weeks back by asking:

"As you look back over your life recently, is there anything else you haven't yet mentioned that may have left you with any residual feelings?"

This question is like a net cast over the whole past before the dream occurred. The net is drawn in, checking if there is any catch from the previous day which had not been found. Ullman calls this a general *fishing question*.

Separate the wood from the trees

Though it is important to remember every detail in a dream, it can be an obstacle especially for people who have a tendency to meticulously analyze all the details in their dreams without having the capacity to *separate the wood from the trees.* They may get so caught up in small details that they fail to understand the bigger picture of the dream. We have all seen trick images, also called "Magic Eye 3D stereograms," where this feature is demonstrated. Typical for these pictures is that when we step further away from them, so far that the details melt together, we see clearly the emerging "big picture." In the most skillfully made Magic Eye images, details disturb us so effectively that the wholeness is almost impossible to see at close range, but amazingly easy when seen from further away.

Can you see the word "Skeema" in these Blobs?

I dreamed of being accused without cause, and this accusation had been publicly spread. I did not have the slightest chance to correct the accusation. Nobody was truly evil, but only completely confident of their own judgmental ability in this matter. Being completely defenseless, I was very distressed.

Every part of this dream was unfamiliar to me, both landscapes and people. After reflecting on all these details, I had become none the wiser for it. Then I stepped back, further away from the details, listening only to the emotional tone of it. Then a memory from my youth flashed through my mind. I had been entirely and unjustly humiliated in public because of a misunderstanding. At the very moment I remembered another, similar predicament, which had taken place shortly before this dream, making me severely distressed for days thereafter. Again, totally without cause on my part, and again, because of a grave misunderstanding. These two incidents caused the same feelings as my dream. I understood that I had never fully recovered from these two incidents, not even from the first one, which had happened decades ago. I managed to find this connective emotional element only after I had turned my attention away from the details, whose intriguing unfamiliarity had locked my attention away from the emotional side of the dream. This mental "big picture" operation reminds me of going behind the opalescent, frosted glass usually seen in bathroom windows, showing only a blurred, holistic vision of the dream moving on the other side of the window, only its emotional outline visible. The visual details of this dream remained a mystery even after this emotional revelation.

Investigating symbols and feelings

Countless dream "cookbooks" do symbol interpretation a disservice, giving the distorted impression that exploring symbols is the most essential prerequisite for dream exploration. This does not hold true. Symbol exploration is only one part of a much more extensive and multifaceted exploration.

Exploring dream symbols is usually easier than exploring the feelings dreams evoke. Feelings are often more elusive, like misty veils, blurred and contradictory in nature, whereas symbols are often quite clear visual images. For a beginner, there is an extra difficulty in recognizing feelings because there are two kinds of feelings: primary feelings belonging to the dream and secondary feelings born *after* the dream reflecting the attitudes toward it. A typical and familiar example is when a dream seems to be very comical. When working with dreams, it is advisable to keep these secondary feelings from contaminating the feelings belonging to the dream.

Both symbols and feelings must be explored and evaluated to maximize the chance of discovering the dream's authentic contents, therefore all feelings must be noted, and every symbol and metaphor studied, leaving no stone unturned in the whole dream. "What general and personal message could exist just inside this symbol, in this feeling?" Even images that keep repeating themselves through many dreams should be explored each time they occur because they always contain something new. By immersing oneself with all senses into the dream landscape, more and more feelings and associations begin to surface with closer examination of the dream's whole sequence and minutiae are revealed that originally went unnoticed.

If we cannot recognize and peel off feelings from inside the images and create a safe atmosphere where these feelings are able to flow out of their symbol shells, then the dream remains closed, because dreams are feelings transformed into living images, or, as Ullman describes them, metaphors in motion. When we are successful in this work, the dream manifests itself as a bodily feeling, as an aha! experience—this is the dream's own voice and language.

Staying with the dream

Freud emphasized the importance of free association. Therapeutic work can last years and consists of many additional tasks other than focusing on patients' dreams, and so patients could be turned loose to associate (e.g. meditate on and meander through trains of thought, feelings, and memories) wildly and freely through all levels of their lives. In this kind of work, associations can lead anywhere; they could lead so far away from the dream that the dream itself finally fades away into the background. This kind of loose association cannot be used in dream work, alone or in the group, because there would never be enough time for it and the dream's own voice would remain unheard.

Associations are also important in practical dream work, which focuses only on the dreams, and not on the dreamer's whole life. Even then, they cannot be allowed to gallop loosely around for too long. The dream must be the focal point from which we make short excursions along the criss-crossing and meandering paths of associations, but then we must return to the dream again.

Problems when working on one's own

Surroundings

The most usual and understandable obstacle when working without the help of others is fatigue and exhaustion. When alone, it is more difficult to stay with the dream when every so often one's thoughts wander off to other matters.

Home is the most typical environment for a lone dream worker. There, other family members quite often manage to interrupt the dreamer's concentration. A totally quiet and tranquil place is essential—the chances of understanding a dream are maximized when the dreamer dives into the dream so deeply that the physical environment almost disappears from the dreamer's senses. The more successful the dive, the more the dreamer's mental state interacts with the dream, increasing the information received from it. On the other hand, the risk of falling asleep is maximized, too! The task of finding the best balance at the narrow border between sleeping and waking is not easy. Diving as deep as possible and coming back to the surface with a live catch from the depths of the soul—finding the best equilibrium between these two states—is a question of both craft (proficiency in the art of working with dreams) and talent. Talent is inborn. Craft has to be learned.

Dreams have no messages

It is easier to change our surroundings than to remove our mental barriers. Especially when exploring dreams on one's own, there are increased odds that we will unintentionally choose the explanation of the dream which is most pleasant and advantageous for our waking ego, thus employing dreams as our attorneys for the defense.

For some people, it is tempting to assume that very strong, forceful dream visions are sent to us from higher forces. In a way, this is true, but if we perceive dreams as coming from some conscious, god-like higher powers, we may develop a dependence on them, believing that they always contain higher, conscious wisdom that guides, protects, and advises us, sending us dream "messages." When dreams are elevated to prophetic levels, it becomes increasingly tempting to see them as higher truths, untouched by all earthly attempts to evaluate them.

This kind of dream worshipping does not have much to do with open-mindedly receiving dreams, but is more like following the reflections of mirrors distorted by our need to find an authority, which saves us from using our own evaluation ability in this complex world. It is always a short and easy road to self-deception, letting ourselves believe the things we want to be true instead of what is actually true. Dreams are not *consciously* wise, but their wisdom is *a state of innocent wisdom*. They do not present solutions, but only our true situation in life, which we have not yet seen clearly enough.

One example where the real solution was found is in a dream where *the dreamer was assiduously cleaning up her yard while her friend was sitting lazily in her garden swing, sipping her drinks, benefiting shamelessly from her generosity.*

This dream depicted very clearly the dreamer's distorted relationship with her friend, but no solution to it. She realized afterwards that *to see the situation clearly was the solution in itself.* Her twisted relationship with this friend had been normalized completely by itself. This kind of solution is the best one: to suddenly see what really *is,* without any conscious effort. These kinds of insight stories are abundant, especially in Zen literature, but often they extend to the whole life of the person, not only to one small part of it as in the dream.

A similar "instant human relation" solution happened in a dream group where a group member, unbeknownst to the dreamer, had been irritated with the dreamer for a long time. They were workmates, belonging to the same workgroup. After hearing the dreamer's dream in the dream group, he understood the reasons for the dreamer's behavior. His irritation toward the dreamer vanished immediately. The solution for the problem was found, but not in the dream, which only illuminated the dreamer's situation. The solution took place in the group member's waking mind after hearing the dream—much like my solution came to me after hearing the tale of the two telephone poles in my first dream group. Nothing else was needed. To see what *is,* is the highest form of solutions. This is also an illustrative example of how dream group supervision may improve workplace atmosphere.

Guiding and counseling dreams

Throughout our lives we have to search for our own individual equilibrium, troubled by all kinds of fears, doubts, and feelings of guilt: should I trust that person or not, do I confess my love, should I change my job, should I marry/divorce, should I tell it like it is or remain silent, am I able to be a good mother to my children, do I have the energy to take care of my old, sick, difficult parents, do others think I am charming or annoying, am I a capable leader, am I an alcoholic, should I confess or hide my shame, and so on, ad infinitum. Year after year we meet an enormous amount of different situations where there are no clear answers that free us from consuming energy by fruitlessly raking over the past and being afraid for the future. Every night these unsolved problems are painted onto our nightly dream canvas again and again, always with new, artistic colors and combinations.

Dreams which seem to be completely positive from beginning to end may create the impression that they are validating the dreamer's lifestyle or waking life solution to some problem, especially so if they contain strong emphasizing elements like affirmations, assertions, and encouragements. Particularly for a dreamer who cannot get second opinions from others, it is dangerously easy to believe that even one's dreams justify and defend the opinions and solutions of one's waking life. Encouraging elements in a dream are especially treacherous. Even a single "certainly" or "of course" in a dream signifies that somewhere the opposite of the encouragements is hidden. The mechanism is very simple: if there were no opposite forces in the play, there would be no need for any reassurances.

The ambivalence created by two opposite forces is one of most typical causes of dreams, even if one of these forces—the one which is more unpleasant to a dreamer—is not immediately visible. When listening to dreams, I often have an image of two horses pulling the dreamer in opposite directions, the poor dreamer torn between these forces. Our life is full of situations where there are simply no right answers, no complete solutions. If we do not manage to solve the emotional tension caused by them during the day, our ambivalent feelings get dressed into nightly images when we continue our search for the best solution or compromise in our dreams, trying to keep the pointer of our balance-scale on zero. We are dreaming like pearl oysters, growing our string of dream pearls around the irritating grains of sand in our daily lives.

One dreamer was, in her dream, an especially efficient worker, and a deep sense of satisfaction from a job well done was as strong in her dream as in her waking life. This dream seemed to validate her view about the right choices made at her job in her waking life. In this dream there was also another person who kept on asking if the dreamer really was able to cope with her job. The dreamer always answered with a resounding *yes*.

Reflecting on her dream, she recognized that the querying person was a manifestation of a growing worry about herself, which she had managed to exclude from her consciousness, and even from the dream, by projecting her worry onto another person. Despite her great ability to complete every task thrown at her, this performance was possible only by consuming her energy to the last drop, and this dream revealed that she was more afraid of suffering a nervous breakdown than she could ever have believed in her waking life. Once she understood her ambivalence better through her dream, she attained a more realistic view of the outer limits of her energies.

One dreamer was encouraged in her dream to go on with her water-skiing. The fascination with speed was intoxicating, just as at this dreamer's job, where she gathered social rewards one after another because of her high competence and efficient activity. On closer examination of the dream, we found details that revealed her anxiety of sinking and drowning, because she knew somewhere inside her that she could not continue at her current pace without burning out. She was literally drowning in her work. Working was like a drug to her, overtaxing her strength. She was a workaholic. The dream contained both positive and negative feelings, both true, but the positive one was easier to recognize in this dream. The encouragement at the very beginning of this dream already indicated that somewhere there was the opposite force against which the encouragements were aimed.

My own dream was, in a way, the opposite, negative in the beginning, positive at the end:

> *I impatiently pushed some broken mechanical gadget to an un-known, yet also well-known man, who let me understand that he could repair it. Then we started to walk side by side, my irritation with him growing with each step. I began counting the seconds aloud: one, two ... haven't you repaired it yet? Not yet? Not yet? Not ... We turned around and I was overwhelmed by a more con-ciliatory attitude. I tapped clumsily on his shoulder, but a bit too forcibly and I feared he might have misunderstood and think that I wanted to fight. But he remained as calm, as neutral, as stony-faced as ever, walking along completely undisturbed. I forced myself to say to him that I had no hard feelings, and that everything would still turn out well for us. I departed from him. We went our separate ways. I felt greatly relieved.*

Who was this familiar unfamiliar man?

The evening before the dream I had tried in vain to assemble a computer, my frustration mounting hour after hour, my rage increasing with that antagonistic machine. Completely beaten by that cursed computer, I went to bed very angry in the small hours of the morning.

When reflecting on this dream next morning, I recognized the awareness which had glimmered through my negative feelings, signaling how insignificant my rage was, and how it had been unable to expand to and poison the innermost part of my soul. This familiar unknown felt like a part of me, capable of seeing deeper inside me, and competent to reassemble the broken pieces of my inner life after the subsiding of my futile rage.

This silent figure corresponded to the feelings that I have about myself, on the one hand I am a mystery to myself, but at the same time astonishingly familiar. At the brightest moments of my life I have felt adumbrations of that quiet, tranquil, unconcerned living core of myself beyond my personality, beyond every form, which can make itself known to the consciousness only through symbols, not directly. In the dream this silent figure calmed me down, escorting me a little closer toward my true self.

There is all kinds of material which can burst out from many levels of the psyche through dreams, which is one reason why it is wise to evaluate dream contents carefully with the help of both intuition and reason, traveling the middle road between them. One should use both of them, on the one side avoiding indiscrimination masquerading as intuition, on the other being careful not to suffocate dreams with intuition–denying hypercriticism.

Dreams do not, unfortunately, guide, warn, or advise us. They only light up our situation in life, without guiding us any more than a flashlight guides us in the dark. When we see an obstacle in a light beam, we have an opportunity to circumvent it. There is no reason to promote the flashlight to the position of The Guide of Higher Wisdom. There is no reason to shift our everyday responsibilities from our waking self onto our dreams.

WORKING WITH ONE ANOTHER

We may have some degree of success when trying to open our own dreams alone without any helper, but it is usually difficult. When working alone, we try to understand our dreams from the same unfruitful, narrow point of view we had the day before the dream. It did not help *then* to relieve the emotional tension which caused the dream, and that's why it does not help us the next day either. Observing our dreams alone is like observing fine artwork, the sculpture of dreams, only from our own angle, illuminating it only with our one, lone spotlight. The remaining sides of the sculpture sit in darkness.

Two spotlights are better than one

Working with a friend or a therapist, opens more possibilities of understanding dreams than working alone. Consider a dream as an artwork, a fine sculpture. When sharing this dream with another, an additional spotlight is switched on, casting the light of the life experiences of another human being onto this sculpture, illuminating it from a new angle, revealing new sides, new aspects of it.

I will not present here how dreams are put to use in individual, especially psychoanalysis-based, psychotherapies, because the goal of these therapies and the time consumed in attaining their goals are different from the goal of this book: namely, to familiarize the reader with a *practical* method which may be very therapeutic, but is not therapy, and which from the ground up has been created to be used by anyone, not only by psychotherapy professionals.

Likewise, I will not discuss the methods of the big names, Freud and Jung, whom I have presented earlier in this book. Their methods have been born from self-observations and individual therapies, and as such are unsuitable for general use.

One characteristic of working with another person is that the process for only two individuals is not as tied to the length and the order of stages as the group process. In the next chapter, I will present the group process in detail. However, the majority of the principles presented there can also be applied to a mini group consisting of only two individuals.

When working with dreams, it is essential to *maximize safety* throughout the process, even when working with your best friend. Dreams reach the core of the human psyche, which means that you have probably never before descended so deeply into the depths of the human soul together. Without safety this journey cannot be undertaken. I will discuss general safety factors in the next chapter.

The considerations to *present and clarify the dream* are similar to those in the group process. After the dreamer has presented his dream, the clarifying stage follows. This clarifying process can take longer and be more detailed than in the group process, and, unlike in the group process where this stage comes later, you can already start asking the dreamer to associate from every dream image. When associating, remember to stay near the dream and avoid rambling too far away from it. The main aim of the questions is always to understand the dream, not the dreamer's whole life. Totally free association belongs to long-term analytical therapies, not to dream groups. Also try to avoid spending too much time on this stage at the expense of other important stages of the process.

Examine the day(s) preceding the dream to search for the emotional context in the dream; this process is similar to the procedure used in a group process.

Share your own ideas. Your turn comes when information from the dreamer begins to dry up, typically when he has exhausted his own ideas and says "I think it is your turn to say what you think about my dream." Make the dream your own by entering into it with all your senses. Why only now? Why not earlier? Because you should not disturb the dreamer's associations with your ideas as long as he readily associates. The more you think that your ideas are brilliant and intuitive, the more you must be on guard you don't blurt them out before the dreamer is ready to hear them. You are searching for what the dream itself has to say. We are all tempted to expound our own wisdom, preferably sooner rather than later, but try to refrain lest you somehow damage the integrity of the dream with a well-meaning but overeager attitude.

Avoid the authority status. When you bring your own ideas into play, bear in mind that the dreamer, conditioned by a general cultural attitude toward experts, including dream interpreters, may cling dependently to your ideas, trying to apply them to himself at an intellectual level without any real emotional connection to them. When the dreamer comments on your ideas like, "Aha! So *that's* what my dream means," you must immediately disabuse him of any faith he may have in your alleged superior understanding of dreams. You may need to repeat many times that you do not have a teacher-pupil relationship, but rather that you are making a joint, equally shared expedition into unknown territory.

You may well be an expert on the dream group process, but you are *not* an expert on any single dream. You are only a midwife, not the mother who has given birth to the dream. It may be necessary to repeat something like, "My ideas are not interpretations of your dream, but only my own ideas about your dream, as if it had been dreamed by me. I do not know what your dream means. Only you can know that. But my ideas may arouse some more ideas of your own. Only your own ideas are able to lead you to a deeper understanding of your dream."

A woman dreamed twice about her sister, who she had not seen for years. Her sister was living abroad, but the reason for their estrangement was a falling out they had years ago. Because she could not understand why she had suddenly dreamed about her sister after years of not speaking, she wanted to share this dream with her friend. They decided to focus on a second dream she had:

> *The dreamer was in her bedroom. Suddenly she heard her sister coming, and at that very moment her sister stepped into the bedroom. The dreamer was astonished, but also somehow offended at her sister's appearance at her home. She thought that the sister had come again to spoil her party.*

There was no party approaching that the sister could possibly spoil. On the other hand, it was true that in the past her sister had in fact managed to spoil more parties than one by picking a quarrel with other guests.

- Her friend asked open-ended and clarifying questions (more on those next chapter): *Was the place her own home?* Yes, it was.
- *Her (the dreamer's) age?* Her true age.
- *How about her sister, how old was she?* Here the dreamer begins to ponder: her sister was somehow strange, not her true self.
- *Can you describe the sister in more detail?* She was like my sister, though there was something different about her.
- *How was the sister dressed?* The dreamer begins to describe the sister's clothing, and then it began to dawn upon her, that her sister looks like someone from the 80's. Her

clothes are somehow old-fashioned, and her sister seems to be younger than she really is. Especially her hair is somehow strange.

- *Could you focus on the hair? The color, length?* The dreamer finds her sister's hair strange. The sister has never had that kind of hair.
- *Does the hair resemble someone else's hair?* The dreamer falls silent—her sister is like her mother, she has mother's hair and resembles her whole being, even the way she walks! She is both her sister and mother!

In this moment the dream opened to her. In a couple of weeks she was going to travel to her hometown to celebrate her friend's 50th birthday (*the party in her dream*). She had not visited her hometown for many years. There was nothing left there from the past other than her mother's grave. Before the dream, the dreamer had told her husband that she would not have time to visit the grave. Now it dawned upon her how strong the feelings associated with that grave were, because her relationship with her mother had been as difficult as that with her sister. That grave seemed to invite her to come and at last put to rest the conflict still deeply engraved in her heart. Her reason for refusing to visit her mother's grave was genuine and understandable—she really did not have time—but it activated this strong, emotional conflict, which threatened to remain unresolved indefinitely.

She understood that she had resurrected her mother to remind her of those unresolved, evaded matters, which now, accompanied by tears of sorrow, surged to her mind. She knew that someday she would return to the grave and salve this tender spot within herself. The settlement with her sister had yet to be reached. Perhaps the day of reconciliation would still dawn.

During the whole process her friend remained strictly in the role of a midwife, an assistant to the dream opening process. She offered no advice or instructions as to how the dreamer should act or which kind of decisions she should make. Nor did she try to comfort the dreamer, because it would have disturbed the healing process taking place inside.

The birth of this dream baby was deeply touching for both of them. As an opening flower bestows its scent and beauty on everybody within its range, so too does the dream.

Another example of a two-person voyage into the dream world took place in a hospital setting. A severely ill patient had had a nightmare, which launched an anxiety attack for which she wanted help.

> *One after another the patient's children and husband come to her, asking who the patient holds dearest in her heart. The patient repeats to each of them that she holds all of them in her heart and loves them equally. The questions continue incessantly, until the patient at last screams at them: "LEAVE ME ALONE!"*

This was a terrifying nightmare for the patient because she pushed away her whole family even though she treasured them above all. This was true the other way around, too. She had always been a most beloved and adored mother, always caring, having excellent relationships with all of them.

When asked for her thoughts and feelings about her stay in the hospital, I began to notice that her account contained more and more similarities with the dream. The longer I talked with her, the more obvious it became how greatly her beloved family exhausted her with their visits. Her life was slowly draining away, but she tried with her last drops of energy to continue to be the same loving, caring mother she had always been. She could not consciously accept her new position of being extremely ill and weak. It was impossible for her to make known to her family that their expressions of love were now unwanted. Her family unwittingly continued to push her into a state of deeper exhaustion.

Her dream depicted her real situation with painful clarity. It illustrated in a touching way how we small human beings in this wide world may fall into impossible situations with each other, even though nobody is evil, even though everybody is loving and well disposed to each other.

After you have gone through the dialogue with the dreamer, stimulated and enhanced by your mutual ideas, the final stage can begin. It is called *orchestration:* a composition and offering of your own ideas on the dream's significance to the dreamer, based on the material you have managed to gather at earlier stages. The orchestration stage is not always needed, as in the previous example. When the process has ended, you can get valuable information from the dreamer by reflecting together on how he experienced your approach.

Later, I will return to the question of how to listen to other people's dreams in situations where it is impossible to resort to any proper dream session, either one-on-one or in a group. These types of situations arise most typically in everyday gatherings where dreams are often discussed, such as during coffee breaks, where our invisible behavioral rules usually exclude the possibility of talking seriously about dreams.

CHAPTER SIX

DREAM SHARING IN A SMALL GROUP SETTING

TWO ESSENTIAL FACTORS FOR A FUNCTIONAL DREAM GROUP

A significantly more effective forum for the exploration of dreams is a small group of about five to ten people, rather than one or two. Each individual and his or her life experiences function in the group like spotlights, illuminating the dream from unique viewpoints, thus creating a more comprehensive and accurate impression of the dream than would be possible with only one or two people.

Because a significant amount of information in a group is conveyed through nonverbal communication, a traditional physical group setting, where the whole group is in the same place, is essential, compared to a plethora of remote gatherings that are never able to fully convey the unspoken nuances in the form of feelings or emotional tones of words and gestures criss-cross. All this is needed for the dreamer to find the tracks that lead toward the essence of the dream.

The safety factor. The group, especially the dreamer, needs an atmosphere of trust and safety. If the dreamer feels he cannot fully trust the group, he will be on guard, thinking twice before saying anything, especially about the dream. Then we can say goodbye to an understanding of the dream. To avoid this we must take many safety factors into consideration.

The discovery factor. Safety alone is not enough. We need elements that maximize the possibility of discovering the dream's innermost core. This means approaching the dreamer's innermost sanctum, which in turn demands that the safety factor must be simultaneously operative. I will discuss safety and discovery in length along with the group process. To the best of my knowledge, the factors needed for understanding dreams are best implemented in Montague Ullman's experiential dream group process. For those who want to go more deeply into practical dream group work, the most accurate and extensive manual is *Appreciating Dreams—A Group Approach,*[47] which represents the crystallization of his life's work. There is also an abundance of republished articles by Ullman at his website *www.siivola.org/monte.*

MONTAGUE ULLMAN'S EXPERIENTIAL DREAM GROUPS—THE MOST POWERFUL TOOL FOR UNDERSTANDING DREAMS

Dream group definition

Ullman said that an experiential dream group is one in which people come together for the purpose of helping each other work out the feelings and metaphors conveyed by the imagery in their dreams. It is an exercise in dream appreciation, analogous to the appreciation of the metaphors in poems. There is no *a priori* theoretical base that guides the response to the images. Dream appreciation places the emphasis on the *feeling response* that comes with the recognition of the connections between the metaphorical dream image and the relevant life situation of the dreamer. Once these connections are made, the dreamer's relationship with the image changes from one of mystery and estrangement to one of relief and appreciation. The group acts as a catalytic agent, supporting the dreamer in the role of expert in relation to his dream.

Ullman often used the following metaphors for a dream group:

- The group functions as a *midwife* to the dreamer by help-ing to deliver the dream into public view.

- The group is a *horse whisperer* who does not scare away the wild dream horse, but tames it to serve humans in mutual respect and understanding.
- The group members are *blind detectives* and therefore do not have direct access to the scene of the dream mystery. They do have, however, their collective experience, and, guided by the dream, they exchange thoughts about possible clues in the hope of helping the dreamer shed some light on the mystery.
- The group is a *curling team*, which with their open-ended questions sweep the ice in front of the gliding dream stone, being very careful not to validate their own view (pushing the stone), but only to clear the path in front of it so that the stone goes along on its own momentum.

The history of the Ullman dream group process

I mentioned earlier how Ullman began to use the concept dream *appreciation* instead of dream *interpretation*. Yet it took two decades before the dream group process was born.

In 1972, Ullman had been a director of the Department of Psychiatry at the Maimonides Medical Center in New York for twelve years, and was concurrently director of the Community Mental Health Center for five years. At that time, the recently-opened Psychological Institute of the University of Gothenburg in Sweden was looking for someone trained in psychoanalytically-oriented psychotherapy to teach. In 1974, Ullman, who had become tired of administration, saw the opportunity to make the transition from administration to teaching. With twenty eager students, he started the course on dreams at the Psychological Institute.

Since the 1950s, the customary way of teaching a clinical course on dreams at the psychoanalytic faculty was to have one of the students; the candidate therapist describe a patient's dream, give a summary of the therapy, and focus on what the dream was revealing about the patient and his transference. Ullman wanted to see how far the class could go with less information: students were given only the age and sex of the patient, the duration of therapy, and the dream's manifest (perceptible) content. Only after ten to fifteen minutes of study were the patient's background and the therapist's ideas about the dream revealed.

Initially, the students reacted with skepticism. Their doubts dissipated when they saw the presenting student's positive reactions to the wide array of ideas that they had produced. The group felt stimulated by the way they were helping the dreamer. Many ideas, which the presenter had not himself thought of, were directly applicable to the dreamer's life situation.

Ullman's next move was to have a live dreamer (one of the students) in the room. The advantage of this was that a broader range of information was made available by the presence of the dreamer, increasing the possibility of making more significant discoveries about him. However, this procedure deeply exposed the dreamer's psyche in a forum setting, which was completely different from the typical "strictly confidential" patient-therapist arrangement. Because of this, ensuring extra safety measures was essential. The student was to work on his dream only to the extent of his own curiosity and interest. The sharing of a dream would be voluntary and no one would be penalized for not doing so. Thus, the safety and discovery factors were built into the process from the beginning. The emphasis was on the *art* of dream work rather than on the *clinical* nature of a therapeutic relationship.

The result was the evolution of the group process during 1974–1976 in a way that far exceeded Ullman's initial expectations. He became more and more convinced that safe and effective dream work could be taught without special psychoanalytic techniques and without any meta-psychological (beyond empirical evidence) theory. He later wrote in a letter to me in March of 2000, "[During my thirty years of conducting dream-sharing groups] I have seen people grow emotionally faster and more dramatically than anything I ever encountered as a privately practicing psychoanalyst." The experiential dream work had demonstrated to him that our defensive structure is more elastic than he had originally thought during his psychoanalyst career. He saw how resistance melted away once the dreamer experienced the support and stimulation of the group in an atmosphere of safety and trust. He understood that during his psychoanalytical career, the patient's resistance to therapy was not caused by patients alone, but also by the therapy itself with its rigid basic assumptions, which had partly choked the dreams' deeper contents.

When Ullman left Sweden in the spring of 1976, he had received enough invitations from professional organizations in various cities to launch a program in Sweden that would continue for the next twenty years. It consisted of visits of six to eight weeks over the next decade and a half, followed by shorter visits from then until 2002. The Swedish Dream Group Forum (*www.dromgruppsforum.org.se*) was established by a small group of Swedes in 1990. At the beginning of 2010 it had 111 members, of whom 32 were certified dream group leaders and 22 were certified dream group supervisors ("leaders of leaders"). The corresponding Finnish Dream Group Forum (*www.siivola.org/surf*) has no official organization or members, but instead works mainly through Internet, and conducts an annual three-day dream seminar and a one-day winter seminar. When I was writing this in the spring of 2010, Ullman had already left us; he died on June 7, 2008, at the age of 91, after holding his last dream groups at his home in Ardsley, New York, only some months before.

Setting up a dream group—you can do it yourself

From now on when talking about dream groups, I mean explicitly Ullman-type experiential dream groups, unless I indicate otherwise.

Reading a book about dreams without participating in the real process is like reading a menu without tasting the food it describes. You cannot sense the taste.

Even if participating in a dream group is the easiest way to learn an effective dream group process, I wish to emphasize that *it is indeed possible to start a dream group without any previous dream group experience.* As a matter of fact, the most active dream group leaders in Finland started groups exactly like that. You can find more resources for starting your own dream group at the back of this book.

Selecting a dream group leader. Ullman did not want to create a specific dream group leader training program with detailed course requirements, examinations, and certificates. The qualification of a dream group leader is not a matter of having completed formal studies, but a question of the character and general life experience. Ullman was not against examinations and psychotherapy trainings, but he emphasized that even though the experience gained from them can be useful, they by no means guarantee that a trainee with all his or her certificates would be a successful dream group leader.

However, Ullman did accept the Swedish dream group leader and the dream group supervisor training courses. He was one of the founders of this Forum in 1990. It is the only organization in the world that grants training certificates for leaders who use his process. The description of this training can be found (in Swedish) at *www.dromgruppsforum.org.se Utbildning*. Training completed under the auspices of the Finnish Dream Group Forum is recognized by the Swedish Forum on an individual basis.

There is an unfounded, very regrettable fear that it is somehow dangerous to start one's own dream groups without having gone through long training. This disservice to dreams derives its origin from the unfortunate history of dream exploration, which has scared people away from their own dreams. It is true that a beginner cannot lead a dream group as skillfully and flexibly as an experienced leader, but the thing to fear is not the dream, but rather the domineering leader who, by believing that he knows the dreamer's dreams better than the dreamer, misuses his authority. There is no need to master everything at once. Only your groundless fear makes you think you must. You do not have to go through every stage of the process immediately. Take your time without burdening yourself too much by attempting to learn the "right" process straight away.

The leader has a double role, both as leader and as participant— also sharing his or her own dreams—in the group. The leader's role diminishes with time when the group learns the process and understands the importance of general responsibility for each other in the group. The process is shared without any interpreting authority, and the leader is guiding only the process, not the others' opinions about the dream. Interchanging the role of leader and, afterwards, evaluating the different leading styles together speeds up the learning process for everyone in the group. Even in the case of very experienced groups that no longer need any leading, it is advisable to nominate one group member as timekeeper, thus freeing others from this task.

The composition of a group. A group can consist of persons both familiar and unknown to each other, young and old, men and women. On average no composition is better or worse than another.

Ullman and I have taken people into our dream groups without any screening. It is extremely rare that this causes difficulties. I recall only five occasions in the last 30 years when I had to stop the group process in order to explain the principles to the participants and we were always able to continue the process afterward. A few times, Ullman asked a group member to stay behind after the first gathering to explain privately that he or she seemed to need more individual help than the group was able to give. On the whole, though, any combination of people works well in the dream group process.

The easiest way to form a new group is to let someone else do it. This someone is an active and interested person who is asked to gather together five to ten friends or colleagues, who in turn, if the group remains too small, can gather their respective friends.

Understanding dreams in a workplace. When holding dream groups at the workplace, there are a couple of special situations where screening of applicants may be desirable. It is usually not sensible to have superiors and their subordinates in the same group.

Caution should also be exercised when a workgroup is placed under obligation to participate in a dream group, say, for example, if a dream group is utilized as a form of group supervision, and participation is mandatory. You, as a dream group leader, should not agree to this arrangement. It is not uncommon for some individuals in a workgroup to dislike or even hate each other. It is easy to understand what kind of havoc this might cause in a dream group. Persons who have a tense relationship with each other should avoid coming to the same group, because it may worsen the atmosphere and make the dreamer cautious, which in turn means diminishing the chances of understanding his dream. A dream group is not the right place to try to resolve serious conflicts.

It is also possible, in the case of mandatory workplace participation, that there will be members who have indifferent, hostile, or frightened attitudes toward dreams. This can make it difficult for the group to work well together. On the other hand, those who do not believe in dreams at all, but are curious about them and want to learn more are positive candidates for dream group work.

Therefore, it must be made clear that only those interested in dream groups should participate, that there will be absolutely no sanctions on those who choose not to, and that everyone is aware beforehand of all participants in their group, so they don't get stuck with someone they don't get along with.

Because supervision-based dream groups are implemented because of problems originating at work, it is sometimes asked if dreams recounted in dream group supervision should be work dreams, or at least dreams with images that connect to work. They need not be because we can never tell in advance from a dream's manifest (perceptible) content whether it contains work themes. In my experience, the majority of dreams without any work images contain important work themes anyway.

Begin with friends. It is easiest to become acquainted with a dream group process by first practicing it with friends. I began my own first group just in that way. I had already participated in some of Ullman's dream groups, but I was too shy to start up my own before my friends gently forced me to begin. The first time was so inspiring that it was easy to continue. If the task of leading a group feels too challenging, you do not have to attempt it alone; your whole group can participate and advance one step at a time by reading instructions and negotiating what to do next. Then, when you feel more versed in the process, you can practice leading the group alone. Of course, you can pause the process anytime and briefly reflect with others on how to proceed. Why try to jump to a too-high a step at once when it can be done just as well with small, easy steps?

A dream group is not a dream therapy group. As such, it is not a substitute for therapy. Dreams *can be* extremely therapeutic and have a faster and deeper influence on the dreamer than even a long-term therapy. I have personally seen it happen. A dream group is suitable for complementing ongoing psychotherapy because it does not have any interpretation system or hidden agenda that could drive a dream group onto a collision course with therapy. Despite its high safety level, however, a dream group is not suitable for psychotic or unstable persons. Intensive immersion into the dream world may be too much for a person with an inherently weak ego structure.

Size factor. The optimum size of the group is five to ten members and six to eight is ideal. If the group is too small, members may feel obliged to make a contribution because of social pressure, even if they only wanted to listen to the process without active participation. If the group is too big, it does not reach the intensity typical of smaller groups.

Time factor. It takes time to work effectively with dreams. The most ideal situation is when there is no defined time limit at all, but rather the process is allowed to follow its own natural rhythm until it ends accordingly. Usually it takes more than two hours to process even a very short dream. Reserving three hours for the process seems to be the most suitable time frame. But if need be, the process can be compressed into two-, or even one-hour sessions, but at the expense of efficiency. Unlike a motorcycle, the human psyche cannot be accelerated to full speed immediately. It takes a considerable time to develop the required atmosphere to encourage intuitive processes in all participants.

Notes are important. I will treat them in more detail after presenting all stages of the group process. Taking notes during these stages is closely related.

General principles for maximizing safety and discovery factors

In order to help the dreamer as effectively as possible, the group must take care of two essential aspects: the *safety factor* and the *discovery factor*, which are essential factors for a functional dream group.

Maximizing safety

Before the actual dream group process starts, the most important *safety factors* must be clarified:

Confidentiality. It is forbidden to relate dreams shared in a group to any outsiders, even when the dream worked through does not seem to contain anything worth concealing. Of course, the dreamer can recount his dream to anybody.

The dreamer monitors his own safety level. Dreams often contain topics that are too intimate to be shared even in a dream group's confidential and safe environment. The group cannot know in advance where the dreamer's closed, sensitive area begins. Even the dreamer does not often recognize these sensitive areas until the process is underway. For this reason, the dreamer must be briefed well in advance that it is important to signal clearly to the group if they begin to come too close to his inner sanctum. If this is not done, and the dreamer and the group senses that maintaining the safety has failed, the entire group can experience, at its worst, heightened anxiety levels and diminished spontaneity even at future gatherings.

Throughout the whole process, the responsibility of protecting the dreamer belongs to the whole group, especially if the dreamer is somehow shy or too polite to raise the STOP sign that informs the group it has gone too far. If anyone in the group senses this has happened, he or she should simply ask the dreamer if this is the case.

Everyone in the group must be protected. The process may raise strong feelings in any member of the group. Especially in new groups, safety is the leader's responsibility, but regardless, the group should be informed at the very beginning that *each group member is responsible not only for the dreamer, but for everyone else in the group.*

If the dreamer already knows *before* sharing the dream that it will contain parts that absolutely cannot be shared then it may be better not to share it at all. Because the theme which may be pivotal for understanding the dream must remain untouched, the group may end up in the stressful situation where it must advance as if in a mine field, without any clear idea of how far it should or is allowed to go.

The dreamer remains in charge. The dreamer can stop the process at any time. This is an "emergency brake," which the dreamer can pull at anytime, or for *any* reason, even if the group and the dreamer do not understand why. The leader has no more authority than others in the group to continue the process. It should be checked, however, that the dreamer has not stopped the process because of a simple misunderstanding. In the latter case, the process can be continued after straightening it out, but of course, only with the dreamer's permission.

The dreamer's willingness to advance to the next stage in the process must be ascertained. It is not necessary to ask mechanically every time if it is clear that the dreamer wants to continue, but if any doubt remains, the dreamer must be asked.

Tactfulness. Some group members may be aware of sensitive and painful matters in the dreamer's life, which the dream seems to reflect, but if the dreamer does not talk about them, then neither should they be touched on by others. If uncertain about the degree of privacy, a group member can check with the dreamer, for example, by passing a note asking if the matter can be disclosed.

No need for verbal contribution. Everyone has total freedom to contribute or not to the discussion. This concerns especially dream sharing. No one should, for any reason, urge another member to share a dream. Everyone must have a complete freedom of choice to share or not, without the influence of others. One has the right to remain silent throughout the whole session, and despite this can learn much from the process.

Maximizing discovery

In their own way, all stages of a dream group process promote discovery. Together they constitute a multifaceted, multidimensional review of not only the dreamer's dream and the time preceding it, but also group members' life experiences. The latter function as catalysts, maximizing the discovery factor. The essential aspect of the dream group process is that all members dive as deeply as possible into the dream, living it, experiencing it with all their senses. This immersive approach invokes in each member feelings from their own lives. Despite all our differences, the basic feelings each of us have on our road through life are similar. Dreams reflect specifically this common area of humanity. By immersing ourselves into the dream, we open the door to our souls, meeting each other in an intensive way. This maximizes the discovery of dreams and what is the most authentic in us. This is the essence of healing.

In order to really maximize our discoveries, we must remember that a dream group seeks only to understand a dream. It does not use the dream as a door through which to step into the dreamer's whole life, as therapists do. *Playing therapist in a dream group is forbidden!* The group must stay with the dream from the beginning to the end of the process. This may sometimes be a bit hard for experienced psychotherapists, who may slip back into their routine approaches and concept systems, shifting their attention away from the dream.

It is essential to understand how totally central the dreamer's role is. The key to the dream is not in the theories of dream authorities. It is found solely in the dream at hand. The dreamer is our only source of information on what the dream means to him. There is no democratic one man-one voice principle, but the group is in the service of the dreamer. This means listening carefully and attentively to everything the dreamer has to say during any and all stages of the process.

There are moments, especially in the dialogue, when it is not always clear if the dreamer is silent because he does not have anything more to say, and is waiting for the group to comment, or because he is searching for words to express his feelings. In the former case the group should break the silence, which may be uncomfortable for the dreamer. In the latter case the group must remain silent to avoid interrupting a crucial train of thought needed to understand the dream. If there is any uncertainty about the dreamer's silence, the dreamer can be asked if there is anything more he wants to say.

The dream group must be attentive to more than just the dreamer's words. A great deal of information is passed between the members via non-verbal communication. Every pause, gesture, and feeling the dreamer conveys contains information, which is not transferable through words alone. All these messages sent by the dreamer should be captured with the group's intuitive antennae. The possibility for maximum discovery is obtained only in an atmosphere of maximum safety where the dreamer feels free to let everything flow without constraint from the depths of his mind, without feeling the need to be on guard, or to censor and tidy his words. The balance between safety and discovery factors is always delicate.

Distracting the dreamer with one's own ideas is easy and should be carefully avoided. It happens in various ways. Some group member may be deeply affected by the dream, because underneath our superficial differences we human beings are quite similar, after all. The dream may tell much about group members' own lives, helping them to understand both the dreamer and themselves. On the other hand, a group member may be so overwhelmed by the dream that he becomes absorbed in his own life situation for too long, disregarding the dreamer. Or, because of the effect on him, he may repeatedly try to offer his own views, despite the dreamer's repeated rejection of his ideas. In the worst case, he may begin to give advice or comfort to the dreamer.

Another human trait that occasionally leads to premature and over-eager suggestions is simply a desire to share one's own fine ideas before some other group member hits on them and takes the credit. In other words: pride and ego. Don't let it take hold, as it has no place in a dream group. Members are there to support the *dreamer*, not to posture their own ideas.

Thus, in order to hear the dream's voice, *we are not allowed to impose our own ideas on the dreamer*. Not until the last stage of the process (called the orchestration stage) are we allowed to offer ideas to the dreamer. Even during the orchestration stage, imposing (which is interpreting) is not allowed. Our offerings are only our own projections, our guesses, our hunches, presented in such a non-demanding way that the dreamer can easily accept or reject them.

Especially during the playback stage, the group presents many questions to the dreamer. The questions must be open-ended, i.e. they must not contain ready-made answers. For example, the question, "Is the man in your dream your husband?" is an obviously imposing question, as it already contains the desired answer.

Similar types of questions are multiple choice, such as, "Is the man in your dream your husband or your son?" Adding more choices (your husband, son, brother, etc.) does not help. All these questions are demanding, forcing the dreamer to take a stance that may not even approach the essence of the dream image in question, but instead force him away from the authentic answer. The preferable, open-ended way to ask a question is, for example, "Is there anything more you would care to say about the man in your dream?" This question does not contain any ready-made answers.

The same useful principles can be applied everywhere in our waking life. An illustrative example of this is perhaps the most common question through the ages and cultures: "Do you believe in God?" It is clearly a demanding question containing ready-made black & white alternative answers. Regrettably, the questioner is usually not interested in hearing a detailed answer, and will draw superficial conclusions about the respondent based on a simple "yes" or "no". A question like this reveals more about the querent's need to sell his own yes-or-no approach rather than to listen. It is easy to understand how richer and more authentic information can be elicited with a question like, "Is there anything more you would care to say on this matter?" Our lives are full of encounters where we could understand each other better by posing non-demanding questions.

The questions we present to the dreamer must be *information eliciting, not information demanding*. Every question posed must be an instrument offered, not one that demands an answer. Demanding questions are "hard" questions that push the dreamer against the wall. For example, the question "why?" is not as harmless as one might think. By asking "why?" we demand the dreamer to find *the cause* of his dream images. Usually the dreamer does not have the slightest idea *why*, and now our question pushes him against the wall by demanding something he does not know, raising his anxiety level.

Group members should not suggest words or ideas in situations where the dreamer seems incapable of finding the right expressions. By suggesting words, the dreamer is open to suggestion and prevented from finding the only correct words for what he is feeling. We have effectively obscured those words by influencing him from outside. It is always better to calmly wait for the dreamer to find the right words without distorting them with our well-meaning helpfulness.

The motives of questions must be transparent to the dreamer. If the dreamer does not understand why a question is presented, it may raise suspicion and mistrust. "Why is he asking that? What ulterior motives does he have? Which theories is he developing? Is he trying to view my human relations as psychologically abnormal? Does he think he's my therapist?" Among the most devastating questions to ask without explaining your motive is, for example, what the dreamer's relationship with his sister is, or, worse still, if the dreamer has ever felt sibling jealousy.

Professional psychotherapists are the most prone to asking questions with hidden motives because they may have routinely used this kind of approach with their patients. This is fine in some forms of psychotherapies, but it is forbidden in dream groups where there are no hidden theoretical agendas, conceptual systems, or technical manipulations. The dreamer is not a patient and the leader is not a therapist. Unlearning old, deeply ingrained therapy habits may take some time, even for veteran psychotherapists.

Group members shall not relieve their anxiety at the expense of the dreamer. When the dream activates a strong emotional reaction in the dreamer, it may at first seem paradoxical that you should *not* go and *comfort* him. This is because it can seriously *disturb the dreamer* just at the moment when the dream is most effective in the healing process. Comforting would be like pushing your own dirty fingers into the wound, preventing the dream surgeon's healing knife from operating. Dream insight is always a healing, integrating operation, even if it stirs up an emotional thunderstorm. The air will always be clearer and fresher after the storm has subsided. Nothing else is needed but a gentle, quiet pause for the dreamer until he is ready to continue the process again.

Another practice to avoid is giving good *advice* to the dreamer in the form of maxims and guiding principles that are effective in our own lives. The dreamer almost always finds this kind of external help disturbing and inapplicable to his life situation.

The stages of dream group process

Earlier, I described many matters worthy of consideration when working with dreams, either solo or in pairs. I will refer back to some of them in the context of the group process. The following detailed stage-by-stage description of this group process should be mastered thoroughly. When first conducting dream groups and practicing to be a leader, it can be useful to use this description as a cheat sheet during meetings.

The process may appear so peculiar and complex that it could raise the question of its relevance to real life. Shouldn't the discussion be free-flowing, spontaneous, without being limited by rules and stages? A novice dream group leader may feel bewildered by all these different stages of the process.

Every stage is necessary, though. A spontaneous discussion tends to shift the focus from dream, wandering off time and again to unessential topics. The constricting rules of everyday communication do not help us to dive from the surface of ordinary social interaction to the depths of living dreams. Therefore, these rules must be changed. We need specially honed communicative tools and a safe atmosphere to illuminate the dream from complementary angles. When we have acquired a deeper knowledge of the profound nature of the human soul through this process, then, of course, this knowledge will enrich all our human relationships.

The structure of this process can be likened to a protective fence around dream flowers. We cannot command the flowers to blossom, but we can protect them against cold winds and from the trampling feet of humans. If we are gentle and caring, then they may open before us in all their full glory.

The Dream Group Process

STAGE 1: PRESENTATION OF THE DREAM

1A   *Listening to the dream*: the dreamer presents only the dream, *not* his ideas about it, nor the events preceding the dream.

1B   *Clarifying the dream*: the group asks clarifying questions in order to obtain a more detailed mental picture of the dream.

STAGE 2: THE GAME—PLAYING THE DREAM

2A   *Projecting feelings*: The group makes the dream its own, putting themselves in the dreamer's place and describing what they feel. The group communicates *only with each other* (*not* with the dreamer, who must be totally undisturbed in this stage, only listening to the group).

2B   *Projecting metaphors*: The group shares their metaphors, together with their feelings, with each other, but not with the dreamer.

STAGE 3: THE DREAM IS RETURNED TO THE DREAMER

3A   *The dreamer's response*: The dreamer associates freely, and must not be interrupted in any way by the group.

3B   The dialogue between the group and the dreamer:

   1   *Searching for the recent emotional context* particularly in the day preceding the dream.

   2   *The playback of the dream*: The dream is read back to the dreamer scene-by-scene, who is then invited to add further ideas from each dream scene with the help of the group's open-ended questions.

   3   *Orchestrating projections (The group's ideas about the possible connections of dreamer's dream imagery and her waking reality).* Using the information obtained from the dreamer, the group members offer their views on the dream's meaning to the dreamer as suggestions, not as interpretations. Members then listen very carefully as the dreamer validates or rejects these ideas.

STAGE 4 : THE FOLLOW-UP

   The dreamer shares any comments on his dream at the next group meeting.

We will now go through these stages in more detail:

Presentation of the Dream (1)

If the group has gathered before, the group, including the dreamer, is asked if they want to comment on the previous session. It is not uncommon for the previous process to have sparked many ideas, which have flamed into new insights. Optionally, if anyone in the group wants to present additional comments to the dreamer he may do so, but only if the dreamer is willing. Ullman refers to this as a delayed orchestration.

After this initial stage, the new process begins by asking if someone has a short and recent dream to share. A short dream is generally preferable, especially in the first session with a new group, because it takes extra time for a leader to delineate the process. The more recent the dream is, the more clearly the dreamer will remember the day before the dream, which improves the chances of finding its connections to the dreamer's daily life. When a group is experienced, it already understands the mechanism of linking the previous day's emotions to dreams. It becomes less important to demonstrate it, and even very old dreams can be shared.

One of the many safety measures taken is that everybody decides alone if he or she would like to share a dream. It is not allowed to ask a particular group member if he or she has a dream to share. This question must be addressed to the whole group. It may otherwise put an individual member into an embarrassing situation, if he has a dream he is unwilling to share. So the prohibition from urging an individual to share a dream, which at first glance may seem to be of minor importance, proves instead to be one of the numerous safety regulations that are unconditionally necessary to protect the dreamer and the whole group.

If there is more than one person eager to share a dream, there are four main factors which need to be considered: 1) how recent the dreams are, 2) the length of the dreams, 3) how recently and frequently the dream candidates have shared in previous sessions, and 4) the dream candidates' eagerness to share. The candidates can negotiate with each other who will share their dream. If the decision still proves to be difficult, then the group lets Dame Fortune make the choice by flipping a coin or drawing lots.

All kinds of dreams can be worked with, even those that are old and long. This choice applies mainly in situations where there are no new or short dreams available, or if some other factors speak in favor of using an older dream. Ultra-short, very diffuse, gray, or dull dreams are also fine, because it is impossible to know in advance which treasures they conceal. The essential emotional core of dreams cannot be deciphered from their manifest content. If the dreamer has two dreams from the same night or two dreams from two different nights that might be related and wishes to share them, they can be worked with if they are reasonably short and there is enough time available.

Listening to the Dream (1A)

When a dreamer is chosen, he then tells his dream and *only the dream*, nothing outside of it, such as his own ideas about its meaning or about the day preceding the dream. Everything the dreamer remembers about the dream should be told in its entirety, not only the most interesting parts. Nor, even if long, should the dreamer shorten it.

Why this restriction? To maximize the effectiveness of the play, which is devised to extract information not from the dreamer's life, but from the group members' lives. If the group already knew at this stage what had happened in the dreamer's life before the dream, and the dreamer's opinions about it, the group would no longer be in a position to create rich, abundant ideas based only on the dream itself, concentrating their attention too much on the dreamer's personal life and ideas. This might be detrimental because the most significant dimensions of the dream may be located in a completely different area than the dreamer believes. This initial restriction heightens the chances for the group to discover these areas invisible to the dreamer.

I recommend group members write down the dream word for word; few people have so good a memory that they could remember the dream exactly. Every forgotten or wrongly remembered word diminishes the chances of understanding the dream.

Clarifying the dream (1B)

In this stage the group has the opportunity to clarify the dream in order to reach a more focused view of it. It always pays to present some basic questions, like time frame of the dream (present, past, future, mixture of these, timelessness), the ages of people in the dream, dreamer included, their clothing, their relationship to the dreamer. Are the places familiar? Are the dream people real people? If yes, do the dream people have any differences compared to real-world people? What colors were in the dream? What emotions and feelings, including dream people's? If the dream contains objects or landscapes that are difficult to explain, the dreamer can be invited to make a rough drawing of them. Any additional clarifying questions can be put forward.

This clarifying stage is, in a way, only a technical one. The group tries to reproduce the dream in their minds as accurately as possible. On the other hand, the group should not devote a disproportionately long time to this stage. Spending 10 minutes or so on this exercise is appropriate, depending on the dream and total time available. It is not uncommon at this stage for the dreamer to remember more details and to begin to have more ideas about the dream's deeper levels.

The game—playing with the dream (2)

Stage 2 is perhaps the most surprising for novices because any communication with the dreamer is forbidden in this stage. The reason for this is to create a reserved area around the dreamer, where he is able to immerse himself in the dream totally undisturbed, listening to ideas criss-crossing between the group members and taking note of the emotions and thoughts this discussion catalyzes in him.

There are two reasons the dreamer should take part in this discussion: if he remembers any additional details of the dream, he should share them immediately with the group, because any detail could be the crucial one for opening the dream in the later stages. Also, if the dreamer detects that someone has misunderstood something in the dream, this should be rectified. The group's contributions must be based on the dream, not on their own modifications.

Every group member steps into the dream, takes the dreamer's place, lets the dream belong to each group member. They are now the dreamer, trying to dive as deeply as possible into the dream with all senses, seeing the dream's landscapes, hearing the dream's voices. The dream is also everyone's dream at the linguistic level: the group is reporting what they are experiencing in the dream in the present tense and in the first person singular. Often group members begin their contribution here by saying "if this *were* my dream..." I want to emphasize here that the dream *is* his dream now, no conditional words needed!

In a way, the group tries to induce a self-hypnotic state by putting their souls into the dream so completely that their physical surroundings and their views as external observers disappear as completely as possible. This role is like an actor's role: total identification with, total dedication to the role, otherwise the process remains shallow, unauthentic, and without spirit. Instead of some cool, theoretical, external, logic-driven opinions about the dream, this immersion is an essential ingredient in helping the dreamer to open the dream.

It is of great importance that everyone in the group understands this. If one person does not identify with the dream, but remains as an external observer, he does not reveal every idea that occurs to him, but filters away those ideas he thinks are relevant only to himself. He reduces the number of his ideas, mentioning only ideas he believes the dreamer will identify with.

This is a *disservice* to the dreamer. In this stage of the process the dream does *not* belong to the dreamer, but to the group! Novices tend to have difficulty accepting this, being afraid to say something the dreamer would not accept. In other words, they have not yet understood the idea of a dream group, thus refusing to help the dreamer. When the group lets all their feelings and metaphors flow freely, reflecting each member's unique nature and life experiences, all this material will trigger additional feelings and ideas in the group like an advancing avalanche, rambling and branching out to weave a rich network matrix.

The keyword of this stage is *richness*. The most important thing is to produce the maximum amount of feelings and metaphors, however conflicting, contradictory, and inconsistent they may be. The group is not preparing any official, unanimous announcement for the dreamer, but is playing with the dream like children, having a fireworks display of sparkling ideas. The dreamer will decide what to choose and ignore from the rich banquet the group has prepared.

In this stage, despite making the dream their own, group members who knew the dreamer before do not have to try to filter out that knowledge. However, they must remember that if they know some painful and sensitive facts about the dreamer, they are *not* allowed to disclose them to the others, regardless of how much the dream seems to refer to those facts. If the dreamer opens the door to these sensitive areas, only then is it permitted for others to step in cautiously. Safety first!

Projecting feelings (2A) and metaphors (2B)

Stage 2 of the dream group process is divided into two parts. The group begins by searching for the emotions that the dream awakens in them. After awhile, the meanings of the metaphors are included in the search. Both are shared with the group, everyone building on each other's ideas.

Why not save time and begin to search for meanings simultaneously with feelings? Because it is easier to find words for metaphors than for feelings, which are often vague, inconsistent, and approximated with words only with difficulty. A novice group especially may slip easily in to the examination of metaphors only, forgetting the importance of searching for feelings. The importance of feelings is emphasized already in this early stage because the main task of the process is to unearth the treasure of feelings buried inside metaphors. If there is not enough time for the process, these two parts can be combined, especially in a more experienced group that has already internalized the importance of feelings.

There will almost always be a dream that raises conflicting feelings among group members. One dream image may trigger rage in one, guilt in another, fear in a third, and freedom in a forth. The more feelings the group produces, the more probable is it that one or more of these will resonate with the dreamer's feelings, thus leading the dreamer toward the feelings contained in his own dream images.

The same happens with metaphors. The more the group produces, the stronger the chance the metaphors will resonate with the dreamer. For example, if you considered for several minutes what a horse might symbolize, you would probably have some conflicting alternatives in your list, such as: hard work (workhorse), hurry, speed (trotting horse), power, grace, nobility, oppressed pride (harnessed horse), ridicule (horseplay), freedom from restraint (wild horse), feeling restricted, restraint (horse with reins), being under the yoke, unexpected winner (dark horse), poetic inspiration (Pegasus), emotionality, sexuality, oversexed man (stallion), or hunger/overeating (eat like a horse). You can see how multiple people reflecting on these metaphors could produce many options for the dreamer to identify with.

As an exercise, let's consider a relatively common dream incident: teeth falling out. You may remember that Freud considered dreams about one's teeth falling out, concluding that it could be interpreted as castration, or as a punishment for masturbating. What ideas do you have about it? My own associations are:

- I am completely toothless in this situation.
- As a punishment for biting somebody they come and knock my teeth out.
- I cannot take it, I cannot swallow any more of this, it is more than I can chew.
- I am a nobody, I do not have any bite, any piercing, any cutting power.
- I cannot nourish myself, the task/the bite is too much for me to chew.
- I now have the strength to get my teeth into this task with tooth and nail.
- I have no courage to show my teeth, no courage to fight tooth and nail. I cannot defend myself because I am not armed to the teeth. I look awful, I am an old woman, soon to be toothless, I am no longer attractive to anybody.
- I am long in the tooth, my powers ebb away, soon I will become a cranky, toothless old man.

The previous ideas were not taken from any dreams. When the dreamer shares his dream, we can see that many of these ideas fall away immediately. If the dream depicts a skinny, starving horse, to see powerful sexuality in it demands stretching one's imagination perhaps *a bit* too far. If in our dream we are naked in a public place, it is telling us that we are ashamed of something. But wait, perhaps not. Perhaps it tells us about our tendency to exhibitionism? And what does that word mean, in turn? Or could it be that we are aggressive, wanting to defy stupid laws and orders? Or do we love the idea of being a nudist, a real, genuine human being without being covered with artificial materials that mask our true form? Are we making a personal statement against morality? Or have we perhaps committed adultery, and are afraid of being unveiled? Which motives, fears, and hopes do we really have?

What comes to my mind when I am sitting in a car and somebody else is driving it? Do I sit beside her or in the back seat? Do I know her? A spouse? Is she the driving force in our relationship? Would I want to be in the driver's seat? What is our destination, speed, or the state of the road? Do we have enough fuel? Will the car stop on this steep uphill road? Is the engine strong enough? Am I strong enough? Will we fall off the high road into the ravine? Am I in some kind of dangerous situation? Are the brakes functional? Should I slow down my working pace? What if the dreamer has been in a real car accident where her husband, who she deeply hated, was killed? In that case it would be surprising if her dream did not contain feelings of joy and freedom in addition to feelings of grief, loneliness, and guilt?

Who is the supervisor / umpire / superior / judge in dreams of examination / matriculation / military / legal trial? Who is responsible for carrying out the task? Is the dreamer at last activating himself after delaying and avoiding responsibility? Is he an overachiever suffering from an inferiority complex, repeatedly sitting examinations in his dreams? Is he afraid his hidden / unlawful / foolish actions will be more closely scrutinized? What if the fear of examinations in a dream is not a metaphor of diverse psychological tensions, but a natural reaction against an approaching real-world examination, which would be frightening for anybody? It might be. Or might not.

The phone does not work / breaks down / nobody answers / wrong people answer / telephone money is missing / telephone catalogue is missing / telephone number is missing. Connection is not made. Is it a bad connection on the telephone or with a person? Is my partner angry? Can't I find any way to approach him or her in order to reveal my love / hate / regret / remorse / concern / anxiety. Or has the real-world telephone been acting up with me recently? If yes, could it also have some symbolic meaning for me?

None of these ideas are exactly right for the dreamer, but all these ideas are needed to help point the dreamer as much as possible in the right direction. Predefined symbols with fixed meanings never correspond exactly with the endlessly unique dream situations. There are always some differences. The more we can empty our minds of predefined symbols, the more freely we can produce a whole palette of them, play with them, and build on each other's ideas. But only the dreamer can decide which is the right one for him—or the wrong one. When one thirty-year-old dream, which had haunted the dreamer his whole life, was finally opened after long and intensive dream work, everyone realized that the group had been on the *wrong* track the whole time. If the group had not been intensely occupied with the dream for almost two hours, the dreamer would not have found the *right* track. Thus even "wrong" ideas can help find the right ones.

Ullman says that this stage is only a game, a kind of pump-priming (pouring in sufficient water to start it) exercise, in the hope that some of what the group produces resonates with the dreamer. See how simple this ideation is? You do not have to know anything about Freud, Jung, or any other dream authority. Neither do you need any therapeutic education or experience. There is nothing mystical or professional in producing these ideas. Take any word, any picture, play with it for a few minutes with your friends, and you will see how easily new ideas are born.

Let us continue our dream exercise about teeth falling out, this time approaching it at a biological level. This tooth dream could be the consequence of a visit to the dentist, where the latter has remarked that the aching teeth are going to *fall out* or that he must now *take them out*. And then, at the psychological level again: the dreamer has perhaps heard from his boss that he must *sink his teeth into* his work, and this statement has triggered a fear of not having the teeth (mettle) necessary for the task, possibly losing his job as a consequence.

When the cause for the breakdown of our food processing machine proved to be that the plastic *teeth* of its cogwheel had eroded away, I felt a powerless, *toothless rage* that there was no spare part available and I had to buy a new machine instead. I do not remember having any dream about this real-life incident, but it could have caused a typical dream about teeth falling out. An interesting teeth-falling-out-dream was one that followed the previous evening's intensive discussion about the meaning behind teeth falling out!

The group can never know the limitless variations of the dreamer's personal life. Only the dreamer possesses a key to all this, a key which many times seems to be lost, but which can be found again with the help of the group acting as blind detectives, groping for it in the dark. The cultural influence assists the group in this task. We are swimming in the same sea of cultural symbols that we all more or less recognize, everyone with our own unique, different style. But the main *gestalt* is so often there that it allows us to help each other recognize these cultural patterns both in our daily lives and in our dreams.

Sometimes, even at this early stage, the dream will have already opened adequately. At this point in one such case, the dreamer thanked the group for their work and said that the ideas they shared had helped her to understand her dream. The group was, of course, very curious to hear what she had understood, but the dreamer said that the material revealed was so sensitive that she could not share it. A very frustrating situation! Because of the importance of the safety factor, the group stopped working with this dream immediately. They could see that the safety measures really worked, and the dreamer could be confident that she would never be pushed further than she was comfortable.

When the group's contributions begin to dry up or become repetitive, or the time begins to run out (about half of the total time available—one and a half hours—should be reserved for stage 3), it is time to return the dream back to the dreamer. An even more important reason for going on to the next stage is the condition of the dreamer. He may seem to become bored, or cast a quick glance at his watch, which are all signs that it is time to continue on. He may feel that the group's abundant ideas are more than he can cope with, so he has every right to say he is ready to move on, or to stop altogether as in the previous example. Remember, the dreamer always has the final say, the supreme control

The Dream is Returned to the Dreamer (3)

Dreamer's response (3A)

Stage 3 begins the dreamer's monologue. He has now heard many comments, which have intensified the presence of the dream, lifting its emotional contents closer to the surface of his consciousness. Now his free-length, freely associating response will catch some essential dream elements. (A neatly organized response would miss nuances that can be captured only by free association.) The dreamer can comment—but does not have to—on the group's contributions, on the dream's meaning to him, on the time preceding the dream, on just about anything. This is the only stage completely dedicated to free association.

The group is not allowed to disturb the dreamer in any way during his monologue. Every outside reaction or comment, even non-verbal, draws the dreamer's attention away from the material welling up inside.

The dreamer's monologue does not have to be uninterrupted. *He can pause* to reflect on what has been said, study his notes, or review the dream if he feels that he still has something to say before moving on to the next stage. The group waits silently, patiently during all these pauses. If this is not made clear from the outset, the dreamer may stop too early, wanting to be polite to the group and not keep them waiting.

The freely associating monologue serves to maximize the discovery factor in this stage. The many feelings and thoughts the group's contributions have awakened are often still fragmented in the dreamer's mind, like separate threads. Free association is a nimble tool, darting among these threads, joining and interlacing the associative wefts into a woven fabric presenting the broader themes of his life.

Due to the wildly bouncing associations, the dreamer may seem at times to wander away from the dream on the criss-crossing paths of associations. This is often quite a challenge for two main reasons, the most usual being technical. Because interrupting the dreamer is prohibited in this stage, note taking is difficult if the dreamer is a fast speaker. Notes are important because these associations invariably contain important material, which should be written down extensively. In the later stages, the more we can use the dreamer's *own* words, the more effective our efforts to open the dream will be. Another difficulty is that associations do not have any clear logic and structure, so they may seem less meaningful than they are, especially to a novice member. It is hard to keep one's attention strictly focused on these associations.

Relatively often the conclusion of this stage seems as chaotic as its beginning, but it almost always contains important information about the connections between the dream and the dreamer's life. This will become more obvious in later stages, when the information, still fragmented in this stage, will be better integrated to form a larger, clearer picture.

Of course, the dream can burst open in any stage—or remain closed to the end of the process. One dramatic example of a dream opening in this stage was when one dreamer had a repeated dream of catastrophe. This frightened her because she thought it might be a precognitive dream about an approaching disaster. This dream began to open with increasing force during her monologue. She realized that the emotional focus in the dream did not point to precognitive elements, but were a direct expression of rage inside her, which she had not previously dared to recognize. Now it flashed open to reveal which events in her daily life had caused this rage. The opening was so clear and powerful that after the dream had spoken with its thundering voice, everyone in the group felt that it was no longer necessary to continue the process.

Search for recent emotional context (3B.1)

Now begins the dialogue, the most demanding part of the process, consisting of three stages. About half the total time should be reserved for it.

In the first stage of the dialogue, everyone's searchlights are turned to a new direction: to the day preceding the dream, searching for the recent emotional context, which is one of the important prerequisites for understanding the dream. Irrespective of how much the dreamer has already said about the preceding day in the previous stage during his monologue, this day must still be charted anyway. Usually the dreamer has simply not paid sufficient attention to it. The more the group is able to help the dreamer to recall the feelings of the past, the greater the probability that he will find connections to his dream, because dreams are live illustrations of the previous day's feelings.

The dreamer must be helped to recapture the recent thoughts and especially feelings, which, their tension still unresolved, emerge as dream images the following night. The most important areas to explore are the last remembered events immediately prior to falling asleep. This search can then be widened to the whole of the previous day, and thereafter to an even more extended period before the dream. The last task in this stage is a general *fishing question* which casts the "fishing net" over the dreamer's past, reaching back as far as weeks and even months: "As you look back over your recent life, is there anything else that occurs to you that you haven't yet mentioned that may have left you with any residual feelings?"

There may be several separate emotional processes in the dreamer's life, some of them perhaps long-term. This fishing question catches them so often, that it is advisable to pose it every time. A typical combination of two emotional streams is some difficult problem at work combined with another familiar problem in private life, such as divorce or a serious illness. Because of the excitement aroused by detective work with dreams, the group very often tends to get carried away with only one of these emotional streams, forgetting the fishing question.

I see these emotional streams as thick oil paints flowing from different angles into a large dream container, beginning to mix with each other, forming fanciful colored vortexes, i.e. dreams, on the surface. If, with the fishing question, the group does not discern and separate out these different emotional daytime streams before they lose their individual identities in the dream, then in later stages it will be harder to understand the relationship between the dream and the daily emotional tensions which have caused it.

Ullman has also used the word emotional *residue* in addition to emotional *context* when speaking about these emotional streams. The latter refers more clearly to the ultimate purpose of finding the connections between the dream and preceding daytime feelings, which—unresolved during the day—linger in the dreamer's mind as emotional *residues*. These then express themselves as dreams during the following night. Here *context* is used in the sense of *relationship, connection* to dream. This may give a false impression of the group's task in this stage. It happens quite often that the group tries to offer the dreamer ideas about the *relationship* between the preceding day feelings and the dream, rather than keeping the focus only on the preceding day.

While the ultimate purpose of the whole process is to find this context, the current stage allows *only the dreamer* to express these connections. The group may have already developed many hypotheses about them, but no one should yet reveal their assumptions. The group has not yet gathered all the information it needs, so to offer their ideas at this stage would be premature and could actually be misleading. Our questions must not be *information-offering,* but *information-eliciting.* A more suitable expression to describe the group's task in this stage might be *identifying and amplifying the emotional climate* that preceded the dream.

Playback—reading the dream back (3B.2)

Upon reaching this stage, the dream has already had time to strongly permeate the atmosphere. The chances for the dreamer to make new discoveries in the dream are significantly higher than in the earlier stages.

114

The group's attention is directed back to the dream, which is now recited aloud by a group member. A dream often contains scenes like a play. The dream is read through scene by scene. If there is not enough time, or the dream is very short, the whole dream can be read through without stopping. With plenty of time available, the dream can be explored image by image.

After each scene the dreamer is asked if there is more he can say about it. He does not have to repeat anything he has already said. Then the group may explore the scene in greater detail. Anyone in the group can draw the dreamer's attention to some details by asking *open-ended* and *information-eliciting* questions. One dreamer's attention was directed to an extra (in reality non-existing) door in her dream's workroom: "...something to say about that other door?" This simple information-eliciting question was enough to open the door, behind which the dreamer found strong emotional incidents in her private life. Until that moment the group had regarded the dream as only work-related.

Many group members may already have theories in this stage about the dream's meaning to the dreamer, but revealing them would still distract him from the dream. He might be drawn into considering the aptness of *external* opinions at the risk of possibly losing forever some yet undiscovered *internal* dream areas. The dreamer's internal radar must still have freedom to rotate 360 degrees around his dream's landscape. External offerings about the dream's meaning are like restricting the movement of this radar to only a narrow sector of the landscape; the sector narrowed by presuppositions of group members. Only open information-eliciting questions, i.e. questions that do not offer any hints to the meaning of the dream images, allow the continued full rotation of the dreamer's mental radar. This keeps open the possibility for new discoveries from the group.

My own mental image of the process in this stage is a big dream ball of wool consisting of many yarns, experiential threads from the life path of the dreamer, the ends of which appear here and there on the ball's surface. These ends are the dream's individual images. By drawing the dreamer's attention to them with simple open-ended questions is like gently pulling at the ends of these yarns, one at a time. When the dreamer gets a new association, it is like cautiously drawing the yarn out of the ball. From the first association, a new question about further associations may lead to additional unraveling of the yarn. Now the group advances with additional questions until the threads of associations finally end, and at last they may have managed to unwind long bits of associative threads. These often end with strongly charged personal memories, even from early childhood, directly connected to the dream at hand.

When the dream has been worked through, and nobody has any more questions, the last stage can begin.

Orchestration—composing the whole (3B.3)

Orchestration is the name Ullman gave to the last stage of the dream group process. This word means a harmonious combination of instruments in an orchestra, a coordination of the elements of a dream, a synthesis of all the small pieces to form one fine piece of music. The questioning of the dreamer ends and the group members now offer their own individual compositions on the supposed connections between the dream and the dreamer. These orchestrated projections come from their own minds and are constructed only with the pieces the dreamer has shared.

The process before orchestration has run as follows: the dreamer's creativity has given birth to a melody (a chain of dream images), but it is not yet ready for presentation, heard only as background music by the dreamer, who has not yet understood its emotional content. He has shared this musical piece (dream) with his audience (group). The group has studied it from many angles, and everybody's sensitivity to individual melody lines has been needed to capture the feelings and find the most resonant words to describe them.

In the final stage; the orchestration, the group presents the words they think express the feeling of this melody in the best way. The dreamer is the only one to judge how well the words offered are able to express his music. If the group is successful in this task, a masterpiece has been born: the song, with it words and melody joined harmoniously together, as if they had always belonged to each other.

The earlier stages of the process were dedicated to acquiring the maximum amount of information from the dreamer. In orchestration, this information is finally served back to the dreamer, hopefully in a refined form, enriched by the group's contributions. But why now? Why not in the earlier stages? We do not want to build our orchestrations prematurely on inadequate foundation, like a foolish man's house built on sand. Premature orchestrations may divert the dreamer from the right track, compelling him to evaluate the group's half-baked offerings and to expend valuable time, which should be dedicated to eliciting additional information from the dreamer. The immensely rich poetry of dreams does not open easily to our rational, non-poetic brains that are impregnated with Western values. Because of this we must first collect every last drop of information we are able to acquire from the dreamer. The whole dream group process has been built from the ground up to maximize this information. The firmer the foundation, the easier it is to build orchestrations on it at every level: biological, psychological, societal, even transpersonal.

Orchestration is the most difficult stage for the group, which is often still confused about the dream's deeper meanings. It is hard to produce easily understandable orchestrations when it might not yet be clear what should be offered. Or when the overall picture of the dream is still only vaguely discernible behind the fog, when the group first tries frenetically to sort all the material in its own head. The dreamer can always ask for clarification of unclearly formulated orchestrations. The ultimate goal is to offer orchestrations, which extend over the whole dream, but smaller, partial orchestrations are also welcome.

Machine-gun firing. In the orchestration phase, there is a greater chance that the group will not listen to the dreamer. This may happen anytime, but especially during orchestration because this is the only moment when the group is allowed to voice their opinions on what the dream could mean for the dreamer. The need of the group to test their ideas about the dream is often so burning that the group members do not have the patience to let the dreamer react to what they say, the next group member throwing in his own ideas immediately after the previous member has finished speaking. There must always be at least a few seconds pause between contributions, and only when the group is sure that the dreamer is ready for the next contribution can it be offered. The dreamer's silence may mean that he is reflecting on what has just been said and is formulating an answer. Of course, nobody is allowed to destroy the information, which is just about to rise in the dreamer's mind, by disrupting his train of thought. If the group is unsure about why the dreamer is silent, the dreamer can be asked if he is ready to continue.

The dreamer as a teacher—a question of politeness. Politeness is a double-edged sword. Because dreams contain very intimate, private dimensions, we must be extremely cautious not to hurt the dreamer's feelings. On the other hand, we must advance deeply into the dream. We must find a balance between the safety factor and the discovery factor. By maximizing safety, we may impair the discovery effect. Our everyday rules of polite conduct say that it is not nice to immediately reject another's view. This rule should be unlearned. Especially in the orchestration phase, the dreamer's politeness may have a negative effect. If the dreamer feels that the offer does not hit the mark, he may tend not to answer directly and honestly, but try to find a polite rejection that doesn't offend his group members. Because the dreamer alone, nobody else, ever has a real knowledge of the dream, by being polite he deprives the group of a very valuable opportunity to see clearly that their projections have not yet found the key to the dream. This also has a negative effect on the dreamer, because he notices that the group thinks that they are right when they are not. We all know how irritating it is when we see that others think they know us better than they really do, and we do not have the chance to correct their mistakes.

It is important to make clear to the group from the outset that even if politeness has its rightful place in our communications, it may have a harmful effect in some situations. *The dreamer is our only teacher,* therefore, it is important that he understands his critical role when the group has missed the mark. When we understand the importance of this, and realize how little we know about each other and about life in general, the "negative" feedback from the dreamer should not hurt anyone's feeling. It is a joyful luxury to find ourselves in a milieu where we are allowed to be more honest than is possible in our ordinary, everyday lives.

The demarcation line between interpretation and projection

Ullman said that the group is offering their *projections* to the dreamer, not their *interpretations.* The psychotherapeutically-oriented sometimes ask me how the projections offered can be anything other than interpretations when the group in this last stage is offering a deluge of even more exotic explanations to the dreamer. The difference is not just a linguistic one. The interpreter *does not know* that he does not know. The experienced projecteur *knows* that he does not know.

Note that I use the expression *interpretation* similar to the way I have used it throughout the book, as one who interprets expresses uncovered self-confidence and belief in one's superiority to understand another human being's dreams better than the dreamer.

One of the psychotherapeutic connotations of the term *projection* means transferring one's feelings, thoughts, and attitudes *unconsciously* to another person; in other words, the person who is projecting does not see his or her projections only as projections, but believes that the object person of these projections has all the traits and qualities the projection contains. I suppose that many of us recognize this phenomenon both in others and also, now and then, in ourselves. We are enchanted by someone, because that person has the same qualities as the one we love; or, we cannot stand a person who looks too much like someone who once ruthlessly rejected us, or we accuse someone of having negative qualities without seeing the very same perceptible fault in ourselves.

Projections presented in the orchestration are, by contrast, *conscious* projections. The more the group has had time to see repeatedly that their projections do not resonate with the dreamer, and have learned from these experiences how projections are projections, not truths, the less they have unrealistic fantasies about their capabilities to see deeply into other people's souls. The better we understand how error-prone we are, the less intrusively we are able to present our projections to the dreamer. This encourages the dreamer to relax his polite compliance and to reject the non-resonating projections. It allows his feelings and associations to flow in an increasingly uncensored and authentic way. This increased information about the state of his soul increases everybody's chances to understand the dream. Thus the circle is closed: to know that we don't know is the key to knowing more than ever before.

The *contents* of the projections offered to the dreamer may be very strong and intimate, but they are allowed because the dreamer knows that he does not have to answer or he can say that the topic goes too far into his private thoughts. The *way* these projections are offered should be non-assertive. For example, if after some projection the dreamer is asked, "Do you agree?" then this should be considered inappropriate. It is a variant of the multiple choice question, which forces the dreamer to choose from predefined answers that are almost valueless, born from the demand to verify the questioner's own theory. We are trying to understand the dream, not to plant our theories into the dreamer's head. We ask, we suggest, we guess but we do not *implant (=interpret)*.

The process usually ends when the time reserved for the process is up. The ideal alternative would be to let the process end naturally, unrestricted, at its own, variable pace. To secure this, the group needs a considerably longer time, at least three hours or more.

The group does not always realize when it is time to stop the process, when it enthusiastically goes on despite the dreamer's polite stop signs, such as casting a glance at his watch. The dreamer's pace is the right pace.

Before closing the process, the dreamer must always be given the last word. Of course, he does not have to use this right if he does not want to. Then the dream is closed, and only the dreamer can re-open it. For learning purposes, it is useful to have a general discussion about the process at the conclusion.

Big and small crimes

The stage-specific description of the process is now over, and we return to more general questions concerning the process.

Arguing, debating, and disputing have both positive and negative connotations. They may mean negotiations, where settlement of differences by mutual concessions are sought in order to arrive at an agreement by adjusting conflicting views. When successful, even wars may be avoided. This is diplomacy at its best. Negatively, they may also imply disputing in an angry or excited way. The obsolete meaning of debate is to *quarrel*. The multiple meanings of these words show how difficult it is to find a fruitful balance between different opinions without awakening negative emotions. The distance between neutral and emotionally toned arguments is very short.

These forms of interchange—which are important in all kinds of life situations when negotiating for the mutual benefit of both parties—do not belong in the dream group process. The process is not democratic—the group members are under the authority of the dreamer. Only the dreamer can validate the ideas offered by the other group members about his dream. The dreamer is the only authority, protected from any persuasions. If the group tries to find a compromise about the meaning of his dream, the dream's voice would be largely displaced by external opinions, thus the main goal of the group would be destroyed. Dreams are like soap bubbles, bursting and vanishing by the slightest pushing, arguing, and debating.

Our everyday arguing often contains a grain of mini-violence against others whose opinions we do not want to hear. We are usually unable to notice this violence, we are so accustomed to it. Our life has blunted our minds to such an extent that we do not see clearly how the infinitesimally small, almost invisible discordances we disseminate in our human relationships accumulate in the course of time, wrecking our relationships, separating us from each other, too often leading to loneliness, divorces, homicides, and suicides.

Dreams catch this repressed, darker side inside of us. We are practicing to better recognize it in dream groups. Understanding dreams helps us to see and reduce those small mischiefs we practice against each other.

Blind detectives

Ullman has often compared the group to blind detectives who help the dreamer search for hints about the lost key to the dream, which ultimately can be found only by the dreamer. This may leave the impression that the group is not allowed to challenge the dreamer's opinions in any way. While opinion pushing is not allowed, if this detective group finds some contradictions or inconsistencies in the dreamer's statements, the group can draw the dreamer's attention to them. Not because the group knows better, but because the group does not know why.

For example, the notes the group has written down may unanimously testify that the dreamer has changed some of his statements during the process without himself realizing. The group cannot know the reason for the changes, but it can ask the dreamer about them. It must not dispute with the dreamer if the dreamer has difficulties in believing the group, otherwise the dreamer will begin to defend himself and the process will have been destroyed. The dreamer is being helped, not persecuted! The dreamer may simply have forgotten what he said earlier, but he may also be actively rejecting something personally very painful. Only the kind of attention that inquires but does not intimidate can help the dreamer and the group to understand what is going on.

Another, more typical situation is where the detective group misses some clues when the dream seems to be solved. The dreamer may declare that he has understood the dream, and even explain to the group how he came to this conclusion. As a certification of the authenticity of this insight, the whole group has seen and felt it happen. What more evidence do we need?

The insight has evidently been a genuine one, and if time is up, then everything is fine. But if there is still time and everybody is still enthusiastic, then good detectives should always consider whether there are more treasures to be found. The joy of the first insight may obscure the fact that all dreams are infinite, like life itself. They contain many layers, some of which perhaps still reachable if the group continues its detective work a little longer. There is always more than meets the eye. Dreams are never only *matter-of-fact-dreams*.

We have a tendency to simplify and classify the things we see, wanting to have control over what we experience. We easily forget the parts that do not easily fit. This trend is often visible when the group has found seemingly well-fitting explanations for a dream image without noticing that the image is not *exactly* the same as the real-world object, dead or alive, thus losing the other levels to which these small differences might lead. Why is the dream person's hairstyle different from the real one? Why does he wear a shirt he does not own in real life? Why is there an extra door in a workroom which otherwise seems to be an exact copy of the real room? "There is something odd about my sister... Is it really her?"

These small differences may broaden the scope of the dream from the previous day to the dreamer's whole life. The detective work on these minutiae may open the dream's holographic nature (every small part containing a reflection of the whole) as in William Blake's poem: *"to see the world in a grain of sand / and heaven in a wild flower / hold infinity in the palm of your hand, and eternity in an hour."*[48] It may well be that this detective work does not always lead anywhere immediately, but it may sow some growing seeds of ideas into the dreamer's mind, leading to later insights.

Projection or repression?

At times, a question is raised in the circles of professional psychotherapists as to why the group's projections are considered projections until the dreamer has verified them. Could they be seen as interpretations, which the dreamer refuses to accept because of his repression of unpleasant truths about himself, rather than projections, which the dreamer does not accept because they simply do not fit? This is a question about who is authorized to define the most valid truth. Is it the non-professional dreamer with all his neuroses, or the long-term, skilled psychotherapists who happen to be in the group? The former!

However, it is not important which school of thought wins the competition of explaining the dreamer's refusal. Neither is it important if the dreamer is neurotic or repressive. It is not important how many renowned dream and therapy authorities there are in a group and what fantastic interpretations they might have. Most important is what is *useful for the dreamer.* Everything else is insignificant or harmful. When we are walking through life, the next step of our mental development must be based on the previous one, otherwise we fall down. *That's why the dreamer is always right—even if he is lying!* If he is dishonest (and everyone is, if we look deep enough inside ourselves), he has his own reasons for being so.

We must be careful not to make truthfulness an ideal. It happened once that one group member accused a dreamer of being dishonest. This was one of those very rare occasions when I had to pause the process immediately and make the rules clear before we could continue. Norms and ideals are too often aimed at regulating the morals of *others*, and if we make truthfulness an ethical norm, the dreamer must defend himself against us even more. Our task is to create a safe, *normless* atmosphere where we are allowed to be ourselves with all our faults and blemishes— only then they can melt away.

WHEN A DREAM DOES NOT OPEN—ABOUT THE IMPORTANCE OF DREAM GROUPS' GOALS

Why do we ponder dreams at all? Generally, it is because we want to open their secrets, but often there is another goal which is more essential.

When a dream does not open after working with it alone, it may be irritating but no one is hurt because of it. Group situations are more delicate. When a dream cannot be opened, who is the culprit? Has the group been too insensitive, stepping over the dreamer's privacy border, frightening him? Or is it the dreamer who invalidates every offer the group makes, even in cases where the dream, with its conspicuous symbols, seems to clearly verify the group's assumptions? Has the dreamer intentionally hidden something from the group? Does he take advantage of the group, perhaps to emphasize his own personality? To point out how incompetent the others are? To prove how meaningless dreams are?

If we are searching for the offender, we have lost the essence of understanding dreams. A dream group is not a tribunal. It is more helpful and illuminating to search for the cause instead of the culprit. Everything has its causes, whether they are discovered or not.

It is important to remember that the dreamer's role is relatively demanding. Sometimes, despite the efforts of the group, the dreamer cannot understand the dream. Or, perhaps he understands it, but it contains such intimate material that he is unwilling to share and he is embarrassed to reveal that this is the case. Because of these, or any other reasons unknown to the group, the dreamer may become increasingly anxious: "How can I find material for the group to work with so that they are not disappointed in me after all the energy they have put into my dream?"

The group, too, may become anxious when a dream cannot be opened. They have put forth their best efforts and are disappointed, and possibly even resentful, when the dreamer rejects each of their ideas one by one. However, groups that think this way are forgetting the purpose of the group in the first place, which is to help the dreamer. The more the dreamer senses that nobody expects a fabulous dream-performance or to gain his applause for their first-class sensitivity, then the more freely he can open himself, and the more the group has a chance to understand the dream. And, more importantly, the more everyone can apply the lessons learned in the group to their human relationships in everyday life.

As long as our highest goal is dream opening, the moments of frustration are inevitable, because perfect dream opening methods exist only in empty promises. Complete un-opening of dreams or process-stopping disturbances are fortunately very rare. They are a bit more frequent in novice groups where utter discretion and consideration have not yet become fully internalized.

I can now define in condensed form the most essential goal in the exploration of dreams and life. The goal is not to have a goal, which simply means that one has learned through trial and error that he does not know what life, including dreams, means. It is accepting life as it has been given to us, without filtering and classifying it. It is awareness of the harm that can come from predefined goals, such as compulsive efforts to get dreams opened. This *"attitudeless attitude"* cannot be learned by willpower, and it cannot be taught by any therapy system, but it is born when we begin to notice how predefined goals on the psychical level mark our direction to the known, closing the possibility of finding something new, fresh, and unknown.

Every time a dream is shared is an exciting, intriguing, fascinating detective story, a puzzle, an adventure into the dreamlands given by life itself. We learn something about everyone's mental images. We learn to recognize unspoken clues in our human relationships. Every time we study dreams, we receive pure lessons from life itself, freed from a spider's nest of the one-dimensional debris of thought patterns. Every dream, opened or not, becomes a learning opportunity when we adopt this adventurous attitude, instead of trying to prove that we must successfully open any dream and becoming frustrated with failure. When dream opening fails, the failure took place before dream work started. Failure is possible only when success has been set as a standard, as a goal. Aspiring for success is not important, but aspiring for truth is. They are two completely different things.

OTHER FORMS OF DREAM GROUPS

Millions of websites alienate people from their dreams because commercialism, stupidity, confessional religiousness, and lack of discrimination give the impression that every activity connected with dreams is of inferior value. People are easily influenced by the Internet. But there are opposite examples, as well, including Ullman's own pages on dream work at *www.siivola.org/monte*. The most visible, reasonable online dream organization is *The International Association for the Study of Dreams* (IASD). It is a non-profit organization that supports dream research and arranges study groups and conferences, albeit mostly using methods other than Ullman's dream groups.

Many forms of dream groups are not strictly dream groups, which use dreams as stepping stones to broader psychological, philosophical, or religious reflections. Dreams become displaced by group members' opinions, not originating from dreams, but from daily waking life. This means replacing the most influential elements with less important ones.

There are innumerable groups that have rigid basic assumptions about the meaning of dreams. I call them *confessional dream groups*. The more strictly one has adopted an interpretative theoretical system, the less one is able to see anything which is not concordant with his theory. It was for this reason that Ullman abandoned the psychoanalytic approach.

I have met groups blindfolded with their theories, mostly in occult circles, where dreams are seen as expressions of higher wisdom, as conscious, autonomous entities, belonging to the realms of guardian angels and spiritual teachers.

There are ways to work with dreams that are not so ideologically limited that they twist dreams into a standard predefined pattern. Nonetheless, they limit the dream process in other ways. They may predefine the process by being too restrictive in advance, for example, by having rules that define which parts of the dream the dreamer is allowed to share. A dream is thus chopped and chained up and tied to a leash of a predefined format.

I draw the reader's attention again to the fact that even if the Ullman way seems at first glance to limit dreams, the contrary is true. Ullman's process is a framework built to protect and secure a free and safe playground for a dream to move in its own direction, not in some predefined channel dictated by methodology. It cannot always be avoided that, on an individual basis, the dreamer is pushed in the direction of the group's ideas instead of his own. However, it is even more harmful if these limiting elements are built into the whole system, choking the dream process.

There are numerous "If this were my dream" type groups, where the group borrows the dream from the dreamer. These are half-distant relatives of Ullman's dream groups, the difference being that their processes stop halfway. As a rule, they lack the last three stages of Ullman's process, which are usually the most important parts. Without them, dreams are practically always doomed to remain at a more superficial level.

CHAPTER SEVEN

DREAMS AND SOCIETY

Those who have participated in Ullman-type dream groups know how our reserve tends to melt away once we experience the support and stimulation in the atmosphere of safety and trust the group generates. Our need to defend ourselves diminishes when nobody tries to knock down our fortress walls. Why keep them up when nobody poses a threat to them? This non-defending state is best made possible through dreams, which illuminate the common area of humanity in all of us. There we are able to recognize in each other's dreams the same basic questions, the same predicaments, the same joys and sorrows of life. To see one's fellow man in the same boat on the same sea of life awakens sympathy from all fellow travelers.

When talking about the role of the dreamer, I hope you do not mind if I now use the expression *medium* in its more esoteric sense. The dreamer is, in a very essential way, the only channel through which we have access to vistas, which our waking life eyes cannot see. But the group functions as "mini-mediums," tapping into their own souls to bring forth elements that can be expressed in words only with difficulty. These elements are catalysts, which help to open the dream's "worm hole" that leads to deeper parts of the dreamer's inner universe. Because the dream is the property of one group member only, and this dream alone is our ticket to the intuitive, emotional universe, we must turn our full attention to the dreamer. One could say that this kind of work is too limited because it is so extremely focused on one dream. Yes, it is limited, but what we lose in breadth, we gain in depth. It is because of this depth that dreams are able to illuminate our lives so extensively and surpasses anything we could see without the help of dreams. Thus the dream group, through their dream lessons, is training to revive the intuitive knowledge left unused for so long under the analytical bombardment of hard facts in our harsh, analytical, knowledge-worshipping society.

And then a dream group comes to an end. A jungle of everyday life waits for us out there, outside any dream group. The atmosphere of safety and trust begins to evaporate in the bright daylight of our society. Our reserve returns, our defensive walls rise again, but not as high as before. We have for a moment caught a deeper glimpse into the human soul, and that vision can never be completely erased, thus making us a little more capable of understanding how to come to better terms with our fellow man.

As individuals we can gain much from dream groups, but can dreams get a better, broader foothold in society? Could they possibly become integrated more deeply into society's infrastructures? What can we learn from dreams? Is there some benefit that would assist us outside the dream groups in all our human relationships?

CULTURE AUTOMATISMS

Over time in every culture a group of communication methods developed between individuals, which in the beginning had a meaning. Little by little, as societies changed, these methods became calcified as meaning escaped from them, leaving behind inherited behavioral patterns of thought and action, like empty, lifeless oyster shells. Many of them are called *good manners*. Many traditions have experienced this fate, petrifying into mechanical, robotic rituals, which cannot be broken without feelings of contrition, shame, and guilt, or without punishment from other people.

Living in our own culture, we have been taught since childhood in innumerable ways what is permitted and prohibited. Thousands of frustrations have taught us how to avoid collision courses with the external world. For most of us this slow, gradual process took place almost invisibly, conditioning us to stay almost automatically inside these cultural and sub-cultural limiting fences. We have settled down there, not consciously thinking any more about the electrical fence, which pens us in and is there to give us shocks if we forget our place in society.

These cultural fences protect us from each other by creating behavioral automatisms so that we do not have to meet each other as we really are, but as harmless, well-mannered individuals. Throughout history many cultures have created a number of safe, superficial small-talk mechanisms. In Finnish culture we have developed relatively few small-talk routines. This complicates our encounters with strangers, compared with, for example, Swedish people. I noticed this distinctly during my years in Sweden.

The price we pay for this shelter of established cultural communication routines is relatively high, because it means losing our own authenticity behind our societal roles, not only in the eyes of others, but also in our own. We no longer remember who we really are because the role mask has been stuck to our faces so tightly that we do not recognize our real faces behind it, believing that this cultural role is more or less our true self. The prisoner of one's own culture may dimly recognize that he lives only partially as himself, but only a few have energy enough to jump over the fence. Most others retreat back to the safe central parts of the fenced area, back to our *consensus reality*.

We may be successful in hiding our real nature behind masks during the day, but every night the most authentic part of us tries to get out from this fenced area through an *ethical aperture*. Ullman writes that we possess a unique inner camera, an inherent and indestructible aspect of our existence, an aspect with an ethical aperture that opens more widely when we dream, revealing a bit more of the truth about ourselves. In our waking lives, our ability to see the truth depends on our individual development and social constraints.

Many of us refuse to explore anything that points beyond waking reality, dreams included. Some of us try to understand this world at a deeper level, but to swim alone against the cultural stream proves to be too challenging for most of us. Even if it is true that the never-ending voyage to the remote corners of one's inner space must be made alone, as prophets and sages have done through the millennia, the first part of this journey can be traveled with others who long to know the truth, and who are still able to listen their hearts under the despotism of intellect. Dream groups are one suitable way to start this exploration.

DOMINANT CULTURE AND SUBCULTURES

In every culture there are small subcultures of dream-exploring groups, but almost nowhere have dreams held a prominent position. There are some exceptions. Probably the most well-known is the Senoi tribe in Malaysia, but studies about their alleged non-violence due to cultural sharing of dreams is so conflicting and contradictory that no meaningful conclusions can be made.

In the earlier stages of evolution, non-violence did not facilitate survival of the species. More essential than pondering on one's or others' dreams has been brute force, swiftness, and astuteness, which could fend off the attacks of the neighboring tribes. Securing a community's continued existence required a healthy suspicion of any unknown and deviating phenomena, regardless of where the threats originated.

Even in modern societies there remain many kinds of physical and psychological dangers that threaten to our need to have control and order over our own lives. Dreams continue to reflect them. Dreams are completely uncontrollable, but altogether attractive; we are drawn to them like moths to the flame, like Odysseus to the Siren's call. Because we have no means to bridle them, we are unable to find any tolerable attitude toward them, falling into a hesitative state where our attitudes drift between curiosity and apprehension. It is understandable there is this same apprehensive attitude toward groups which practice dream exploration, effectively barring the integration of dreams into our societies' institutions, especially into education systems and into generally accepted collective values. On the individual level it affects even those who declare that they do not believe in dreams, because irrespective of what they say, even they are afraid that they might, after all, reveal through dreams something shameful or traumatic in themselves.

A dominant culture is a collection of values, norms, customs, habits, and institutions, all common practices which keep society's wheels turning. It represents a demanding, practical, earthbound approach to everyday problems, where there is no time to wait for dreams to solve them. Dreams have no market value, which limits them to endowing their value and beauty only on small circles. They seem to be doomed to live as the Flying Dutchmen, seen at every haven but never able to return to home. C.G. Jung wrote,

> We are so captivated by and entangled in our subjective consciousness that we have forgotten the age-old fact that God speaks chiefly through dreams and visions. The Buddhist discards the world of unconscious fantasies as useless illusions; the Christian puts his Church and his Bible between himself and his unconscious; and the rational intellectual does not yet know that his consciousness is not his total psyche.

Everything has its own place, including intellect and analysis, when helping society to function as smoothly as possible. But if the part of the human psyche that is beyond intellect (and beyond blind trust) is lost, then also lost are the taste and freshness of life, which can be appreciated only by the non-rational part of our psyche. This essential dimension of life has no place in the material core of our society, but is more or less found in dreams, folklores, myths, religions, and their secular versions, i.e. psychotherapies.

THE SUBCULTURE OF PSYCHIATRY

Our interest in dreams awakened during the last hundred years through the psychiatric heritage, beginning with Freud, who understood the importance of the subconscious. Jung followed him, broadening the concept of subconscious to include the collective subconscious. Their conceptual constructions limited dream interpretation only to professionals who had mastered both theory and technique. It institutionalized dream interpretation as a tumor firmly fastened onto the flank of psychotherapy. Erich Fromm stated, "[I]nterpretation of dreams is still considered legitimate only when employed by the psychiatrist in the treatment of neurotic patients. On the contrary, I believe that symbolic language is the one foreign language that each of us must learn."[49]

This tight coupling of dreams with psychotherapies and psychiatry—which impedes bringing dreams out of closed therapy rooms for everyone's advantage—is deeply engraved in Western society. Because a non-professional can hardly distinguish psychoanalysis, psychotherapy, and psychiatry from each other, there prevails a false assumption that dreams are an important tool in psychiatry. Contrary to popular belief, the use of dreams in psychiatry is practically non-existent. Psychiatry has the same view and same blind spots regarding reality as the surrounding culture, which nurtures and provides funds for it. Psychiatry cannot help but deem the phenomena that surpass society's comprehension as pathological. Dreams and many other kinds of altered states of consciousness are seen as analogous to mental disorders. Even Freud, the great appreciator of dreams, considered dreams fundamentally pathological.

A dream group is not a dream therapy group

A dream group may be very *therapeutic*, but it is not *therapy*.[50] Even if psychotherapies may make use of dreams, working with dreams has no more to do with therapy than a car has to do with its driver. Driving a car is not the professional drivers' monopoly, and many drivers do not fall into the category of professional. Dreams are for everyone. The dream group process should not be confused with psychotherapies, and no formal license can guarantee either the competence of the psychotherapist or the dream group leader. Here is a list of the most important differences:

- *No therapist role.* A dream group leader does not assume the therapist's role in trying to recognize and manage the dreamer's possible defense mechanisms. The dream itself is the only therapist present.
- *No background theories.* A dream group leader, unlike a group therapist, does not have any invisible background theories about the group. The motives behind each stage of the process are known to everybody. He is not trying to apply any theoretical knowledge. He is simply an expert in the dream group process, not an expert of any particular dream.

- *No theories explaining dream symbols.* In the unlearning chapter, it became evident how little any predefined assumptions help in the understanding of dreams. Only information emanating from a dreamer is real, authentic information. To hear it, our minds must be emptied of any other noise. C.G. Jung (1948) said: "It is so difficult to understand a dream that for a long time I have made it a rule, when someone tells me a dream and asks for my opinion, to say first of all to myself: 'I have no idea what this dream means.' After that I can begin to examine the dream."[51]
- *No discussion of participants' mutual relationships.* Unlike in group therapy, the relationships in a dream group are not discussed and group dynamics are not examined. These relationships may appear indirectly through dreams, if group members are dreaming about each other, but even in this case the group stays only within the dreams without shifting the focus to group dynamics.
- *No democracy.* In a sense, there is no democracy in a dream group, because it only reflects the dreamer's needs. The others' needs are subjugated to the dreamer's. The dreamer has the greatest influence on the process, and the group must conform to his idiosyncrasies.
- *No discussion of other topics.* A dream group focuses only on the dream at hand. The target area of psychotherapy is much wider, often a client's whole life. A dream, if anything, illustrates the whole life of a dreamer, but a dream group never uses dreams as stepping-stones to other topics in a dreamer's life. Everything said about the dreamer's life must have a clear connection to his dream. This creates plenty of time to examine the dream, and the time typically reserved for a single dream is usually much longer than any psychotherapy session.
- *Thorough dream work.* Compared with individual dream work and individual therapy, a dream group is capable of producing much richer metaphorical material, thus opening up a much broader vista to a dreamer's life.

- *No hierarchy.* A psychotherapist has a hierarchical relationship to clients, even if this hierarchy is not particularly conspicuous. The dream group strives to minimize these dependencies. A dream group leader participates in the process like other members, including sharing his dreams.
- *The role of the leader diminishes over time.* The more advanced a group, the less a leader is needed as his tasks and his responsibilities are shared between group members.
- *Harmful transference effects are minimized.* Transference phenomena are harmful in dream groups because they prevent us seeing our most authentic inner core. In addition, they create harmful dependencies between group members. The dream group process has been constructed to minimize these harmful phenomena.

LIFE OUTSIDE DREAM GROUPS

Most people who are interested in dreams do not reach the critical limit where interest in dreams changes from the temporary to the permanent. They give up because they have not been lucky enough to see the impressive power of opening dreams. As in finance, the return on an investment must be greater than the original investment or interest withers away. Without others' help in the dream group, this limit almost always remains unattainable.

You have already received enough information from earlier chapters of this book that even if you have not yet participated in dream groups, you may already be willing to apply this knowledge in one way or another. You can find guidance on starting your own group with friends on page 91. It is the easiest way to take the next step on the way to understanding dreams.

I mentioned earlier that one of the main goals for dream groups is to take dreams back from the experts and restore them to whom they really belong: the dreamers themselves. This can be done by starting new dream groups. But is there anything else we could do to share the riches of dreams for the benefit of humankind? Could talking about dreams outside dream groups fall on fertile ground when we know how much safety, time, effort, and technique is needed to bring our dreams to bloom?

Dreams outside dream groups

For many years, cultures passed their teachings to successive generations through narrative, but Western mass media and popular culture have been detached from personal, experiential history, of which dream telling has always been a part. Neither one individual, nor even a whole generation, can change the cultural pressure. This makes it impossible to seriously share dreams as a mass activity in our modern society. In American and European cultures, public dream telling is allowed only as entertainment. Even 1618, the French good conduct guide, *Maximes de la Bienséance en la Conversation*, warned to "never recount your dreams in public." The same warning, depicting dreams as "saboteurs of small talk," is found in the 2006 American guide *The Art of Civilized Conversation*.

For this reason, trying to start a serious conversation about dreams is practically impossible in typical "small talk situations," such as coffee breaks, where one has to tread the fine line between empty joking and making a fool of oneself. How about an intensive dream discussion born by lucky chance with a stranger during a railway journey, for example? Or huddling in a corner during a party with someone interested in dreams while others cast quizzical glances your way?

I have emphasized how carefully dreams must be approached, even in situations where all the safety measures are activated. A person telling his dream outside a dream group does not have this kind of safety net, which makes the dream topic still more difficult to manage. It needs careful balancing, like catching a large fish with a very thin line. If you appear too interested in the dream, you draw too strongly on the line, the dreamer takes fright, and withdraws from the conversation. The line snaps, and the fish disappears.

If you are caught in a situation where someone wants to tell a dream, asking to hear your interpretation, do not swallow the authoritarian bait for the prestige you are offered. Instead, ask the dreamer to tell more about the dream, and still more and more. If he is serious, he will continue, and both of you will become more deeply immersed in the dream (this is stage 1B of the group process). But because the setting is far from optimal, and because motivation for this kind of question is usually entertainment, the other's interest often dies immediately after he understands that he will not receive any quick interpretations from you.

The dream group of humanity

The best way to bring the lessons of dreams to all our human relations is still untold. It will be successful only after dreams have taught us that the living core they contain is far from being a separate nightly phenomenon, that their strong undercurrents permeate our whole being day and night. Although they are less visible in our waking life under the bright sun of external activities, they appear no less strongly as maelstroms of feelings, mental and verbal images, and inklings.

We understand increasingly clearly, as if we have never left our dream group, but have only stepped into the biggest dream group of all—into the dream group of humankind. There, among our fellow men, we can apply the skills we have learned in dream groups—the skill to listen, to understand that which we do not understand. Then the most essential matters are not the dreams, which have propelled us toward deeper wisdom of the *"attitudeless attitude," the knowledge of ignorance.* Through these, we learn what psychotherapies, philosophies, and religions have always known: we are all still wandering in the dream states of our day consciousness and our cultures, from which some of the wisest prophets and sages have been capable to wake.

When you listen carefully, asking only open-ended, non-demanding questions, without pushing your own opinions, just as in the dream group, your fellow man may tell you his dreams, fantasies, fears, hopes, delights, his more authentic self. Through the healing joy of having truly been heard, he does the same to you as you have done to him:

> *"For with what judgment you judge,*
> *you will be judged;*
> *and with the same measure you use,*
> *it will be measured back to you."*[52]

CHAPTER EIGHT

DREAMS AND THE UNIVERSE

We are traveling deeper into abysses of dreams and beyond. The deeper our expedition progresses, the more we begin to see connections of dreams with arts and religions, myths and fantasies, and feel instinctively the existence of the source from which they spring. They appear as images, visions and feelings, which our rational mind tries to capture with analyses and classifications.

SOURCES OF DREAM IMAGES

Human life can be divided in many ways. Divided into four levels, the first three are *biological, personal,* and *societal.* The fourth has many names, such as *transpersonal, transcendent, spiritual, cosmic.* If we combine the second and third, we get a simpler division into three: *body, mind,* and *spirit.*

Any single dream can simultaneously bring information from all these levels, intertwining them like oil paints assimilating into colorful vortexes in the human mind.

The first source is biological, of the *body.* All kinds of physical disequilibrium states can initiate dreams, anything in body chemistry and circulation, such as fever, alcohol intoxication, deep fatigue. They occur when the body is reacting to its own stresses, not initiated by mental or psychological activity.

On the next level are *literal* dreams, which *inform* a dreamer by solving everyday problems in dream situations, which do not differ much from waking life. For example, a musician is also training in his dreams for his concert the next day, and a schoolboy for his examination.

The next information level is the symbolic, metaphorical. It contains common themes and symbols relevant to society as a whole, in addition to individual meanings. These dreams do not only merely inform, but *transform* a dreamer. The impact of these dreams is stronger, sending more intense emotions rippling through the whole body. Just as it is not always easy to see the wood for the trees, the societal meaning of dream images may be hard to see at first from inside a society. If, for example, an Indian woman dreams about being a cow, it is easy to see how it could hold religious connotations for her, being in a society that holds cows sacred, than it would for a Western woman with a similar cow dream.

Finally, the highest information level is *visionary*. It contains forceful, high-impact transpersonal, mythological, and religious themes. The intensity of their intuitive insight potential may redirect the dreamer's life in a twinkling of an eye.

CREATIVITY

In our time, the word *art* usually evokes the thoughts of *creativity,* which produces a combination of these two as *creative arts,* the purest form of which is *art for its own sake* without any other goal. It is pure intuition that rationality has not contaminated with all kinds of backstage operations in order to take advantage of it.

Creativity, while creating new forms, resorts as little as possible to any old constructs. Good humor is one form of creativity that is able to reveal surprising, fresh, unexpected views of our life. Creativity in its absolute purest state creates new forms from nothing, not even by combining old creations to make new. The ultimate form of creativity is, of course, the Creator's, who, as far as I know, created the universe from nothing.

Everything obvious, clear, and unambiguous that can be explained is limited and unable to create the new, but only variations of the old. The completely new, as such, must be completely unknown, because if it were known, it would not be new anymore. We human beings are longing for something new, fresh ways to experience this world, something that refreshes the repetitive, dull waking life. But at the same time, we are afraid of allowing what is truly new to flow into our known and safe world, because anything unknown may be dangerous and could irreversibly change our familiar ways of experiencing life. Because of this fear, we prefer to continue in our familiar, narrow rut, our curiosity occasionally commanding us to rise and look over the edge to see what is there in the wide world before our fear takes over again and thwarts these silly plans.

When approaching the origins of creativity, we arrive at the frontier where the kingdom of *creative madness* begins. Salvador Dali is an illustrative commercialized example of this. Creative madness is an interesting expression because of the very contradictory feelings it contains. It awakens mixed feelings of fear, scorn, disdain, and curiosity. It creates in us a longing for something that is at the same time enchanting and bewitching, that contains a promise of freedom in unheard of proportions, along with unknown hazards, being perhaps a one-way ticket to insanity and rejection from our own community. It contains the sad message for the uncreative slave of waking-life, namely that one cannot reach this kingdom by any sensible, normal way, but only by leaving behind any firm and dear opinion, any defense, before the gate to the kingdom of creativity opens.

It is just this ambivalent mixture of curiosity and fear—which is discernible in our attitudes to our dreams—that indisputably demonstrates our own unknown madness to us every night. It depends on the point of view we choose: from the vantage point of waking consciousness, dreams are sheer madness; from the point that understands waking consciousness is not necessarily the highest and only reality, dreams are a creative force from which the finest works of art have originated.

ART AND ART FORMS

No art *form* is art itself, not even the art of dreams. Forms, like dream images, are the mediators of art, which is beyond all forms. Art is the primordial sea, where the waves of art forms arise only to disappear a moment later. Art is a mirror that does not contain any images, only reflections of the artist's own consciousness. Thus, my definition of true art is that it cannot be defined. If it can be defined, it is no longer living art. It is not a boundless sea, but only one wave among innumerable others, eternally raising and vanishing forms. Art is like water, not having a form of its own, but which can be brought to souls that thirst for creativity in a variety of drinking vessels crafted by many kinds of art.

Creative arts always contain potential seeds of an inner, sometimes even external, revolution. The other extreme of socialized art forms is applied arts. Its main motive is to produce, often industrially, objects of utility and function for everyday use. At best, it is aesthetic and soul-soothing; at worst, it is subordinated to the exercise of power. The best-known examples of this are socialist realism and public art in North Korea.

A person who does not feel any attraction to religions, but also shuns a materialistic view of the world may find an outlet for his life between these two extremes, through generally accepted *tamed compromise art*.

THE ART OF DREAMS

The most creative of all art forms is the art of dreams, the oldest, deepest and most authentic. It makes no compromises with our waking consciousness, it cannot be bribed, but it expresses both the individual and collective mental states with unflinching honesty. It is the pure soil of innocence, where conscious forms of art germinate. Countless are the stories of how artists found their inspiration from their dreams.

The art of dreams has the same problem as any other art form: how to convey the living core of a dream to others when even a dream artist—everyone of us—does not know how to make the most of it. We need a craft, tools, a process which we learn to master, like a painter needs his tools, his colors, his brushes, and his talent to attach the shadow of an internal vision to an external canvas. How to tell others about Mona Lisa's smile, how to convey the art of dreams to others so that they do not break into pieces of "right" interpretation in interpreters' theoretical mills?

The more creative an artist is, the less his intellect censors the oddities that rise from the depths of his soul, even when he is awake. The daytime creative process, however, cannot completely avoid bargaining with the external world, leading to compromises. Dream images, unaffected by the desires of the day consciousness, do not pick and choose their audiences.

They do not ask who paid more and who applauded the most. They are not interested in fan clubs and pleasing the critics.

A key in the lock of its society

The task of an artist is to combine the possible and impossible, to give a form to that which is beyond any forms. An art form has to be a thorn in the flesh of a society, not so big that society can pull the thorn out, but not so small that it goes unnoticed. It must humble itself to court a society, just the right amount to attract people to look into the mirror of art, recognizing their reflections without feeling provoked by what they see. Without this kind of compromise, the artist will become isolated or crucified in the turbulence of world history.

As incorruptible as dreams are, sharing them is not possible without compromises, because none of us is very delighted to hear truths about ourselves. Having learned from bitter experiences, we have reason to be watchful. Gaining each other's confidence and creating a safe atmosphere are essential. There are many kinds of keys, but personally, I have not found any better key to open the lock and introduce the art of dreams than the Ullman-type dream group process, which maximizes both safety and discovery factors. The riches of dreams are not situated in the key, which can only open the door; each person must decide if he or she will step through the door into the dream room, but unlocking it is the first step.

COMMON SOURCES OF SCIENCE AND ART

Ullman worked for sixteen years as a psychoanalyst. He used to say that psychoanalysis taught him the art of listening, but not the art of dreams. He felt that applying basic psychoanalytical assumptions to dreams produced interpretations, which are better fitted to theories and which raised patients' defenses rather than lowered them. He wanted to remove any factors that impeded direct observation of dreams. His solution was not to create a new interpretation system, which would have again obscured observation with theories. Ullman's experiential dream group process was built to be as independent from the worldviews and personal experiences of participants as possible, including those of the group leader.

Ullman's reserve regarding all interpretative conceptual systems originated from strange and powerful experiences in his youth, which could not be placed into any known physical and psychological model.[53] These deep experiences helped him avoid conventional explanations about the nature of reality in favor of a greater appreciation of the depth of our ignorance. The transformative impact of his experiences rippled into the rest of his life as he searched for deeper ways to understand the universe. In his books and articles, he reviewed predominantly individual and societal phenomena occurring in dream, and over the course of time increasingly shifted his focus to include transpersonal phenomena.

We will now discuss the realm of natural sciences, especially quantum theory. Although the hard facts of science seem to be diametrically opposed to the world of dreams, it was just in that very place that Ullman found the most suitable concepts to illustrate his thoughts on the deepest nature of dreams.

The similarity of Einstein's and dreams' creative processes

A human being does not often possess a simultaneous capacity both for intellect and intuition. This is seen in the sharp lines drawn between opponents and proponents of these character traits; scientists and artists, materialists and spiritualists, believers and atheists, men and women. Only few are seen to promenade in no-man's land. The capacity for analytical activity of Western culture led to resplendent victories of science and choked the life out of gods, killing the appreciation of intuitive ways to explore the world. It does not need to be like this. The greatest scientists are the best evidence of the fruitful cooperation between intuition and intellect in the same person.

The common source of intellect and intuition is a mystery. Both are needed. Both science and art, intellect and intuition, rational and non-rational united elegantly in one of the best-known and most highly praised scientists of our time, Albert Einstein. He wrote, "The most beautiful and profound emotion we can experience is the sensation of the mystical. It is the sower of all true science. He to whom this emotion is a stranger, who can no longer wonder and stand rapt in awe, is as good as dead. In this sense, and in this sense only, I belong to the ranks of devoutly religious men."[54]

Einstein said elsewhere: "The bigotry of the nonbeliever is for me nearly as funny as the bigotry of the believer." (Goldman, 1997). And "The eternal mystery of the world is its comprehensibility. [...] The fact that it is comprehensible is a miracle."[55]

Einstein's creative process holds striking similarities with dream images. He wrote that in the first phase, words and language did not have a role in his thinking mechanism, which consisted mainly of clear images and signs that he played by recombining and repeating them. Words and other signs had to be laboriously sought in the second phase, after the first phase had been sufficiently established.[56] This playing with mental images and associatively hunting expressive words for them is the main activity in dream groups.

This kind of creative process that translates personal images—which, at the beginning of a process, even the individual himself does not understand—into globally useful applications through scientific and art communities can spring to life anywhere. Creativity does not ask if the individual in question has an official education and credentials in the art of creativity.

Scientist and artists—those professional explorers of inner and outer space—have found new views from their dreams and shared them with others after being freed from the captivity of thoughts that clank on the one-dimensional rails of cause and effect. (It is ironic that being *off the rails* usually means being mad—but here I mean creative madness; the prerequisite for real creativity.) Einstein is said to have dreamed in his boyhood that he was sledding down a hill at night. He began traveling faster and faster, and finally the sled was approaching the speed of light. He looked up and saw the twinkling stars refracted into a brilliant spectrum of colors he had never seen before. Einstein is said to have told science-reporter Edwin Newman, "I knew I had to understand that dream, and I would say that my entire scientific career has been a meditation on that dream."

We can only experience time flowing forward and we cannot exist simultaneously in more than one place. All of us have experienced how our dreams do not comply with these "laws" of time and space. Despite seeming "off the rails," they are in good company with two branches of the hard-nosed natural sciences: nuclear/quantum physics and astronomy, which do not follow any familiar laws, operating with non–locality, complementarity[57] (wave–particle duality of phenomena, for example light), and relative, even backwards-flowing time.

BREAKING UP THE WORLDVIEW OF DAY CONSCIOUSNESS

The worldview of a quantum physicist

Over thirty years ago, Ullman discovered the renowned quantum physicist David Bohm's thoughts about the structure of the universe. Ullman felt that Bohm's concepts best expressed his own reflections. The Western scientific heritage analyzes, classifies, separates, and divides, hoping to finally arrive at the smallest, most indivisible entities the universe consists of. In 400 B.C., a Greek philosopher named Democritus was the most renowned exponent of this school of thought. He created the concept of a particle that cannot be divided and makes up the universe, calling it *atomon* (indivisible). Modern nuclear physics have had time to divide that *atomon* many times, deep inside not only an atom, but inside its nucleus. This interest to divide everything has prevailed in the development of physics.

Bohm noted that for physicists, "the world is assumed to be constituted of a set of separately existent, indivisible and unchangeable 'elementary particles,' which are the fundamental 'building blocks' of the entire universe. [...][T]here seems to be an unshakable faith among physicists that either such particles, or some other kind yet to be discovered, will eventually make possible a complete and coherent explanation of everything."[58] Bohm moved in the opposite direction. He described an indivisible whole where everything depends on the whole like a wave that cannot be separated from the sea. His most-used concepts are *implicate order, explicate order, manifest order,* and *perceptual order; consensus reality.* Ullman repeatedly returned to these concepts in his writings when he tried to describe the deepest essence of dreams.

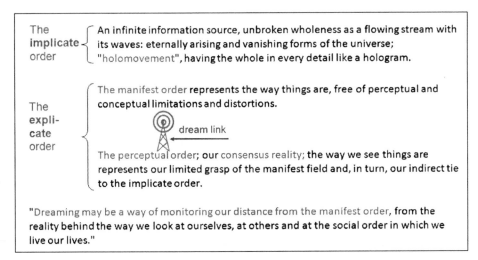

Figure 1: Bohm's orders

The implicate order and religions

The *consensus reality* is the easiest to comprehend because it is a part of our reality that is perceptible to our physical senses. We have a *consensus* that a chair is a chair. This form of reality takes place in our *perceptual order*. Our consensus is relatively limited, though, because in spite of the fact that we see the same physical world, we combine the bits and pieces of our perceptions in very different ways. This is easily seen, especially in political and religious areas, when comparing their innumerable discrepancies in reasoning, conclusions, claims, and arguments.

Next is *the manifest order*, the way things *are*, not as we *perceive* them; our universe is more than we are ever able to perceive. The whole universe is, in a way, within the limits of our understanding, because we are capable of understanding what we do *not* understand. We understand that despite our limited observational apparati (our senses), there must be much in the explicate order that is impossible to sense or even measure with any device.

The implicate order, the ultimate reality, is by contrast totally beyond everything, beyond time and space, beyond the universe. It is the focus, the focal point, the deepest core of religions, and numerous known and unknown religious philosophers have labeled the implicate order God, Atman, Nirvana, Factor X, etc. One typical way to describe it is to define what it is *not*, because what it *is* cannot be described. Because it is not at all inside the explicate reality, it leads us to a chain of negating definitions *ad infinitum*. Among those words used to describe the indescribable, nirvana is interesting because it is a familiar word even in the Western world, who understands it as *nothing,* as a mere emptiness, because it is nothing. This way of understanding it misses the point, because it is not understood that *it is not even nothing,* but beyond being nothing and not-nothing.

This kind of text feels nonsensical, which, seen from the conceptual vantage point, it really *is*. Because language is a bunch of concepts, there is no better way to convey these dimensions than through the pinhole of language. Concepts are finite, and to express the infinite with them leads to paradoxical expressions aimed to derail one-dimensional trains of thought and push them into the abyss of infinity. Paradox exists only on the conceptual level. It vanishes completely when the limitations of thought processes are understood and it is seen that sensible and not sensible exist as opposites only inside the prison of thought processes.

One could think that the implicate order, the infinite, is simply infinite, and there is no need to twist this clear fact with any silly wordplay, but it is deceitful to express the infinite so simply, leading to pseudo-understanding. On the conceptual level, infinite is not infinite, but a finite word invented by finite thought. It is merely a concept that we have attached to something completely unknown. Barry J. Marshall said when receiving his Nobel Prize in Medicine in 2005: "The greatest obstacle to knowledge is not ignorance; it is the illusion of knowledge."

What does this have to do with dreams? If we think of the achievements of quantum physics, we see that playing with the concepts of non-locality and relativity of time have produced the greatest leaps in hard science, beginning with Albert Einstein. Dreams have these kinds of quantum qualities: they expand over time and space. We feel ourselves being pulled simultaneously to different places, being different beings, feeling ourselves young and old, living here and now and in the past or future. We do not need mystical sects to explain this to us, it is all within our reach when we quiet ourselves and begin to listen to dreams and life. Quantum physics functions as a bridging element to broader thinking for a mind that, until now, believed a clock and measuring tape are the most effective tools to understand this world.

Dreams as mediators between manifest order and perceptual order

In our daily lives we are conscious of only that sector of reality within range of our physical senses, our perceptual reality, which we have equated to our "proper" reality. Dreams seem to be somehow more unrealistic than daytime reality. The extreme subjectivity of reality, which opens to our senses, is easy to comprehend with simple thinking and elementary school knowledge about the variety of senses of a variety of animals. Microbes, insects, and earthworms must have a very different conception of the world than ours. Even if we know that they must experience their world radically differently, we stop halfway, thinking that our world is the only "real" world, and the worlds other organisms perceive are only thin slices of our own.

This misconception about the objectivity of our perceptions is quite amazing because the primitiveness of it is so easy to see. We have forgotten, or not even thought about, how many organisms have more accurate senses that perceive things we humans do not. There is no foundation for believing that the perceptual reality of humankind is the highest form of reality. Reality is *always* something more than any perceptual reality, even if the ability of perception of some alleged higher species were a thousand times more broad and accurate than our own.

Ullman hypothesized that dreaming might be a bridge between the perceptual and the manifest order, a way of monitoring our distance from the manifest order (which is the reality *behind* the way we look at ourselves, at others, and at the social order we live in).[59] In dreams, we close the gap between the perceptual and the manifest orders, i.e. we are closer to what we really are. Dreams are like loopholes to broader dimensions from our daytime fortification. Dreams are like wide open ethical apertures into being more fully human.

Ullman's sketch (1974) below represents this mediator activity of dreams between these different types of realities.[60]

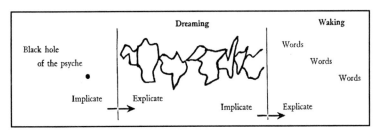

Figure 2: The transformation process in dreaming

Ullman felt that our psyche contains immense amount of information, most of which is beyond our reach; we cannot gain any impressions of it. The black hole of the psyche contains extremely condensed, invisible masses of information. Our waking consciousness directs our attention to the tasks our physical life impresses on us. That's why we need a transformer, a beacon, a link whose messaging helps us discern some glimpses of the deepest information in our souls. In the first stage, the information from the black hole appears at the outer limit of our consciousness. It cannot really appear as such, because it is beyond any conscious perceptions, but it is in the guise of its symbolic representatives, i.e. dreams. In this stage, this dream information is still our private property, and mostly incomprehensible to our day consciousness.

Compare the similarity of this with Einstein's portrayal of the first mental image stage of his creative process. Note also the similarity with Jung's characterization of archetypes manifesting themselves through symbols.

In the next stage, we must make this information visible, transform this private experience into a public one, explicate to ourselves and others with the help of language. But *language alone is not enough because a lot of information dreams contain is easier to feel than explain.* That's why the physical presence in a dream group is essential. Even when the Internet develops to a level where error-free, real-time video can bring together participants from any location, I am still not sure that it would be able to convey all the nonverbal information, the "scent" of dreams.

I return once more to Bohm and Ullman's concepts, placing them in my own figure, which illustrates my view of the position of dream groups in the gamut of human consciousnesses.

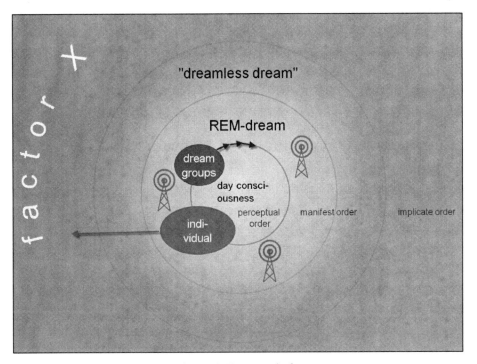

Figure 3: Dream circles

Dream groups rotate around the outer limit of waking consciousness, trying to see more than before, to widen the limiting border between day consciousness and REM sleep. Because dreams are real, strong phenomena beyond our day consciousness, the dreamer gives the group a precious present from beyond, a key creating a possibility to see more deeply through the open gate of dreams than would be possible in waking consciousness.

In this figure, I have placed an individual, in addition to a dream group, at the same orbit line between day consciousness and REM sleep It is possible for an individual to be detached from the orbit through the dream layers to the outer zone of the figure, beyond every form of consciousness, landing in realms of the common deepest "experiences" of humankind, about which religions have, over thousands of years, tried to imperfectly and incompletely explain.

REM dream is like a relay station through which new material from deeper sleeping states is flowing into the reach of day consciousness. Sleeping state is in an important way more real than our day consciousness.

It is a universal accumulator, charging us every night with new energy, whereas our day consciousness consumes energy during a few hours. If the real, concrete energy comes to us through our sleep— the energy-consuming pattern of our physical body is an excellent example—how could our sleeping state processes be less real? The true reality must also be where never-ending, inexhaustible energy fills us night after night.

The projections of dreaming and waking life

I described earlier how subject and object can be merged in dreams. Surely it is easy to understand that any dream must be the dreamer's own, personal landscape, but only when emotions are found inside dream images can we understand more clearly how the dreamer's daytime personality and life situation are related to dream images.

During the day, it is not easy to recognize how completely our world is our own creation. If this knowledge about the total subjectivity of our world is missing, it leads to wondering, among other things, how there can be so many people who do not understand how things *really* are. No one has been able to completely avoid this form of blindness. When someone dreams about a murderer, he does not necessarily recognize that his murderer is likely his own suppressed feelings. These mechanisms are always operative in everyone's subconscious. Our suppressed feelings search for expression through dream images, and in our waking life tend to project those feelings to our fellow men.

The remark "I could kill him," said in humor in the waking state, may be transformed into a killing scene in next night's dream, clearly revealing our emotional undercurrents. Everyone knows someone who accuses others of having faults they themselves are guilty of. More often than not, this poor person is sitting in our own head. After successful dream work, a dreamer may recognize more clearly the murderous man in himself, even during the day, and he will stop accusing others of his own faults, becoming a bit more tolerable for his fellow men.

The sameness of subject and object

We are by ourselves more often than many of us believe. We continue to step further toward the complete sameness of subject and object, and through this discovery it becomes easier to understand why we are always alone in the dream world. I do not mean the kinds of dream interpretation schools that consider every dream a representation of a dreamer without asking who this dreamer is.

The next step is to explore is what this "I," this "me" really is.

I will explain using the sense of sight from among the physical senses.

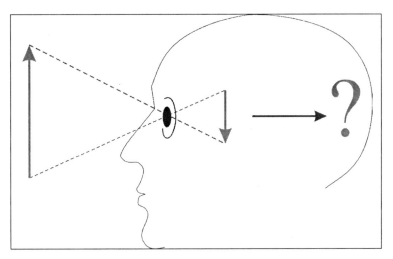

Figure 4: Subject and object in vision

This figure depicts this situation. Now the question is, *where is the border between "I" and the world this "I" is observing?* The initial reaction is usually to draw the border as the outer surface of our carnal body, in this example, the surface of an eye. Where are *you*, the part of you that you feel as "me"? Most people feel themselves, their conscious "me," to be situated somewhere behind their eyes, inside the skull.

Next, the image of an arrow is reflected upside down on your retina, at the back wall of your eye. Now, is the image inside your eyeball a part of you, the "me," or does it still belong to the surroundings, to the outer world? The retina cells in your eye send electrical impulses along optical nerves to the back of your head, where the visual center is situated. Do these electrical impulses traveling through your brain still belong to the outer world, or are they already a part of "me." Or are you somewhere still deeper?

Any border between the observer and the observed is artificial and arbitrary. You may turn your nose at this, thinking the question completely artificial. You may feel that you are you and that's it! Your attitude does not depend on your logical capacity because this matter is much simpler than you can imagine, so if you still have some curiosity left, read on, slowly. We will tie it all back into dreams at the end.

Is it possible to get information about the *real* world? Technically, it has been transformed into electrical impulses in your brain, the combination of which is dependent on brain anatomy. This transformation of incoming information is huge! Instead of the arrow in picture, instead of the world, you "see" only millions of small electrical currents bouncing around in millions of nerve cables. What could be left of the original, of the "real" world? Without this cacophonic firing in your brain, you could not get any visual information from outside. The conclusion is that you do not know anything about the *real world*, which is in fact "real" only in parentheses. Even if the coding system in the brain of your fellow man seems to produce almost the same results, i.e. you both to see that a chair is a chair, it is only a proof of the similarity of your brain coding systems, not about reality. No one has any better information about reality, which is totally, completely, irrevocably, everlastingly unknown.

Many scientists are able to understand that there is no objective reality, but it happens very often that one important piece in their logic is still missing, the absence of which collapses their house of cards. The missing piece is, again, the "me." The key sentence of this chapter about subject and object is: *All observations of yourself are only observations among observations, not yourself.* All observations about the observer and the observed are both only observations, nothing more "real." The information about yourself, about electrical currents in the optic nerves, about the mechanism of the eye, and about the nice lake outside your summer house all have the same value. Knowledge of yourself is not any more objective than knowledge about anything else. Then, what you really are remains a mystery.

This mystery is also waiting for you in your own dreams. You have certainly experienced many times how the unknown has trapped your identity. You have dreamed many times how unknown you are to yourself, speaking, acting, thinking in ways you could never accept in "real" life. You have lost your morals, shunned your ethics, been in two places at once. Isn't all that quite schizophrenic? You feel that your dream "me" is not you, but you know that it *is* you. Or is your dream identity perhaps some kind of possession, created by evil spirits, having nothing to do with you? Or some background noise created by your nightly brain, not you, not worth to spare a thought for it?

Let us reverse this question. Of all the different modes of perception, you have decided that "real me" is the one you sense in the waking state, the one that has repeatedly continued to remain so unchanged over time that you have confused *familiarity* with *reality*.

The problem with mysterious dream experiences being the subject and object at the same time vanishes when we understand that subject and object cannot be separated at all even in the daytime, because they are the same thing. Everything we see in other human beings is inside ourselves and a part of ourselves, vigorously edited by our brain's physical structure. This does not include only human beings, but the whole universe, every distant star, sense of time, all this is us and we, in turn are mysteries. Everything we sense are our *own* properties, a collection of properties, a type of consciousness an organism has needed to develop to survive in its own surroundings during evolution. The development of our consciousness is not a question of understanding the real reality, but of developing the appropriate thin slices of consciousness that have helped organisms survive.

We know how many things can change our consciousness, such as brain injuries, drugs, narcotics, hypnotics, psychological shocks, religious experiences. We know that other persons may have almost completely different opinions about ourselves than we have, and vice versa. In addition to all this, dreams demonstrate the brittleness of our sense of reality when, night after night, year after year, we believe in our dreams that our dream reality is the physical reality. Despite this massive evidence of our extreme weakness to judge which reality we are in and who we are, we always believe that we are in the physical reality, which is for us the only "real" reality.

It is in a way both enchanting and frightening that this continuous massive erring about the nature of reality seems unable to show us that our familiar everyday consciousness is as subjective as our dream state, and that they are only states among many others. When in my dream I believe that I am not dreaming, how can I reject the lesson of this experience immediately the next morning, believing again that the state after awakening is "true," despite the additional evidence that almost all of us have had dreams about awakening? Despite all this evidence from different areas of our existence, the absolute majority of human beings disregard it completely.

What benefit do we gain from this knowledge about the total subjectivity of reality? It may have a tremendously positive effect on our human relationships. If we *really* understand that it is completely impossible to own reality, our efforts to change others' views to be more similar to ours will unavoidably and radically diminish, and our curiosity to know more about other persons' realities will unavoidably increase. We all have experienced how it is good to be near a human being who does not try to change us, but leaves us to be what we are. How much we talk about this, and how little we are able to implement it! As long as we have not understood how completely subjective our notions about reality are, we cannot avoid a collision course with each other, and we continue to be amazed why others cannot understand all the simple truths we have. In the worst case, we may even wonder why only sensible people agree with us!

Through this topic of complete subjectivity (note though that there is no subject), we approach the same practical conclusion about the subject/object problem of dreams described on page 65. Now we expanded this question to include *everything*.

When we understand that there is no one-dimensional scale for ranking states of consciousness, but that they are like a multitude of different flowers in wild meadows, it is better to let all flowers blossom than root up the "wrong" ones. Which one among the infinite patterns of a kaleidoscope of life could be the best? The one where the kaleidoscope should be stopped? When there cannot be any truth, which is the best one? Why irritate others with one's own truths and interpretations? When this insight takes place, the flow reverses, and instead of spouting out our opinions, we are able to be silent and listen to the world flowing into us. We begin to see and hear more. Others cease to be objects for the propagation of our opinions, transforming into exciting objects of investigation: does this other person have some properties of consciousness which I do not happen to have? Could he teach me something new?

False awakenings and lucid dreams

Earlier, I mentioned *false awakenings,* which strongly point to our weak evaluation ability concerning what is "true." Most of us have seen these kinds of dreams; some even have dreams where they awaken multiple times within the dream before "actually" waking up. Or have they? Have we? Is there a series of awakenings, perhaps even *ad infinitum,* and the human race is only on the first steps of this series?

What about the phenomenon of *lucid dreams,* where we recognize that we are dreaming? They are altered states of consciousness, which we can learn from like any situation. An especially interesting depiction of the spectrum nature of reality is C.G. Jung's account of his life-threatening illness. It means that a monochrome belief in absolute reality is replaced by a full rainbow spectrum of infinite variations of consciousnesses. We know many people who recognize only one color, one belief, one truth, despite their dreams' opposite, ever-present evidence.

Relatively large numbers of people, even those who have not experienced other types of altered states of consciousness, have experienced at least one lucid dream during their lifetime; estimates vary that between twenty to sixty percent of people have had one. Unfortunately, they can be used as tools for prestige and power, a dreamer bragging about his ability to enter into such a state. The opportunity to learn as much as possible decreases when a dreamer contaminates the dream reality with negative character traits from the waking state. If you have had the luck to get a passport to the realms of lucid dreams, you would do better to behave like an attentive, observant explorer, not like an intrusive and noisy tourist.

BEYOND THE KNOWN

Our journey to understand and explore dreams in practice draws to a close. Hopefully, the thinness of the dividing lines between dreams, waking state, and other states of altered consciousness has become evident, as well as the deep relativity and subjectivity of all these states. Understanding dreams is, in the lifelong study of reality, only an elementary school, where no admission examinations are needed, and where doors are open every night to anyone willing to learn. From there, we have daily homework, though most of us are not eager to spend our daytime studying.

We have learned about prophets and sages, the connoisseurs of many versions of day dreaming. Through them runs the red thread of religions and not one of them able to declare an exclusive right to reality. Additionally, there have always been, through decades and millennia and countries and cultures, those who report that the nature of reality reflects something immeasurable that surpasses the limits of *both* intellect *and* emotion. The Zen Buddhist laughs at the moon gliding from behind the cloud, the heavens open to Jesus and the Spirit of God descends upon him as a dove, Krishnamurti and Buddha rise up from under their respective trees[61] with a new insight, and Walt Whitman is suddenly overwhelmed:

> Swiftly arose and spread around me the peace and knowl-edge that pass all the argument of the earth; / And I know that the hand of God is the promise of my own, / And I know that the spirit of God is the brother of my own; / And that all the men ever born are also my brothers, and the women my sisters and lovers; / And that a kelson of the creation is love; / And limitless are leaves, stiff or drooping in the fields; / And brown ants in the little wells beneath them; / And mossy scabs of the worm fence, and heap'd stones, elder, mullen and poke-weed.

Once more, I recall one of the most notable dream researchers of the 20th century, C.G. Jung. At the beginning of 1944, when he was 68 years old, he broke his foot, after which he had a heart attack. During the weeks of his illness, he experienced deliriums and visions, the most influential he had ever experienced. He felt it was impossible to convey the beauty and intensity of emotion he felt during those visions. The reality of this experience is of an extremely controversial nature. On the one hand, it can easily be explained away as a sick old man's mental disturbance; on the other hand, it contains interesting ingredients that seem to validate its authenticity. A Western mind wants to control the reality by dichotomizing everything into categories, which exclude each other. Jung's experience is not so easy to place neatly in any typical classification of altered mental states, and just this true/false, real/unreal duality makes it especially interesting. Jung's experiences reflect the spirit of my book, the infinite enigma of dreams and the multifaceted reality that never surrenders to any clear definitions.

Jung begins his account by explaining that he had reached the outermost limit, where he did not know whether he was in a dream or in ecstasy. He felt he was a thousand miles high in space, and far below he saw the Earth. In another direction, he saw a tremendous dark stone, bigger than his house, floating in space like himself. As he approached the steps leading up to the entrance in the rock, a strange thing happened:[62]

> I had the feeling that everything was being sloughed away; everything I aimed at or wished for or thought, the whole phantasmagoria of earthly existence, fell away or was stripped from me—an extremely painful process. Nevertheless, something remained; it was as if I now carried along with me everything I had ever experienced or done, everything that had happened around me. I might also say: it was with me, and I was it. I consisted of all that, so to speak. I consisted of my own history, and I felt with great certainty: this is what I am. I am this bundle of what has been, and what has been accomplished. —This experience gave me a feeling of extreme poverty, but at the same time of great fullness. There was no longer anything I wanted or desired. I existed in an objective form; I was what I had been and lived. At first the sense of annihilation predominated, of having been stripped or pillaged; but suddenly that became of no consequence. Everything seemed to be past; what remained was a *fait accompli*, without any reference back to what had been. There was no longer any regret that something had dropped away or been taken away. On the contrary: I had everything that I was, and that was everything.

His visions continued night after night over three weeks, usually for about an hour at midnight. As he began to recover he thought,

> Now I must return to the 'box system' again. For it seemed to me as if behind the horizon of the cosmos a three-dimensional

world had been artificially built up, in which each person sat by himself in a little box. And now I should have to convince myself all over again that this was important! Life and the whole world struck me as a prison, and it bothered me beyond measure that I should again be finding all that quite in order. —Now grey morning is coming again; now comes the grey world with its boxes! What idiocy, what hideous nonsense!

Those inner states were so fantastically beautiful that by comparison this world appeared downright ridiculous. —It is impossible to convey the beauty and intensity of emotion during those visions. They were the most tremendous things I have ever experienced. And what a contrast the day was: I was tormented and on edge; everything irritated me; everything was too material, too crude and clumsy, terribly limited both spatially and spiritually. It was all an imprisonment, for reasons impossible to divine, and yet it had a kind of hypnotic power, a cogency, as if it were reality itself, for all that I had clearly perceived its emptiness. Although my belief in the world returned to me, I have never since entirely freed myself of the impression that this life is a segment of existence, which is enacted in a three-dimensional boxlike universe especially constructed for it.

As if to underline his attitude toward these visions he stated: "I would never have imagined, that any such experience was possible. It was not a product of imagination. The visions and experiences were utterly real; there was nothing subjective about them; they all had a quality of absolute objectivity." These are strong statements from a scientist who became world-famous for his explorations of the human psyche, especially when we take note that he considered that his visions were caused by his illness. *Real* visions caused by the most *unreal* (from psychiatric viewpoint) mental state! His opinion about the authenticity of his visions did not change during the next 17 years; the rest of his life. Reality and hallucinations intertwine here in an inextricable way, surpassing our dualistic fantasies of being able to separate reality and illusions, dreams and waking consciousness.

Our waking consciousness, despite its utter subjectivity, has "hypnotic power, a cogency, as if it were reality itself, for all that I had clearly perceived its emptiness. Although my belief in the world returned to me, I have never since entirely freed myself of the impression that this life is a segment of existence which is enacted in a three-dimensional box like universe especially set up for it."

This account also illustrates one of the main themes in my book: there is no best way to judge and interpret the value, the authenticity, the essence, the ratio of reality and illusion of Jung's and everyone else's inner experiences. Everyone has a unique personal reality of his own. Everyone experiences and interprets life differently at every level, from individuals to nations. There is no fixed point in the universe, in space, or in time where Archimedes could find his famous fixed place to stand, where he could move the Earth with his lever. Generation after generation seems to think they have found a world-saving, enduring ideology with which they could move the masses, but this will always, sooner or later, lead to wars against those who think they have found it too. The winds of time erased the power of Rome and everything else, leaving behind few traces. The less we have fixed opinions, certainties, and conceptual systems, the more we have a chance to listen and understand others, thus making life a bit easier for everyone. One, only one, of those many places to practice the art of listening, is a dream group.

FROM THE UNDERSTANDING OF DREAMS TO THE UNDERSTANDING OF LIFE

Memories of my old wise friend come back to me. He had already left us before Ullman came into my life. Ullman was my dream master, giving me the tools to study dreams and live life, which have been of tremendous help both to me and to others. My old friend was my master in spirit, but he did not give any practical, teachable tools for the benefit of others. His impact took a longer, more subdued route. He had never participated in a dream group, but had learned his lessons in life through other means. His own dreams played a significant role. He told me that he slept only about three hours of ordinary sleep, consciously examining his own dreams the rest of the time. He, like Ullman, had the uncanny ability to listen to all kinds of people, irrespective of their ideological backgrounds.

In all my dreams and in all my dream groups, my personal goal is the same as both these masters of mine: a burning desire to demonstrate the existence of the road that leads to where dreams are born and beyond. It is the road of the human soul, which my old friend in spirit had personally found. It is the "roadless" road, which each of us must find alone. Even dream groups cannot take us there, but while on the road, we can learn valuable lessons from them about the innocence of the human soul and the unity of the human species. These lessons come to fruition in all our human relationships.

I once showed my old friend the famous ox-herding pictures of Zen, consisting of ten pictures depicting different stages of an individual's spiritual path. After reading it, he said to me in his natural way: "I am in number ten!" This last picture shows the phase when a truth seeker ceases his quest and steps out from his hut, entering the city with bliss-bestowing hands. Both my masters have done just this, in their own way and style. I carry both of those men in my heart, still feeling the healing touch of their hands.

Entering the city with Bliss-bestowing Hands

Inside his gate, a thousand sages do not know him. The beauty of his garden is invisible. Why should one search for the footprints of the patriarchs? He goes to the market place with his wine bottle and returns home with his staff. He visits the wine shop and the market, and everyone he looks upon becomes enlightened.

Entering the city with bliss-bestowing hands
Bare-chested and bare-footed, he comes out into the market place;
Daubed with mud and ashes, how broadly he smiles!

There is no need for the miraculous power of the gods,
For he touches, and lo! the dead trees are in full bloom.

160

EPILOGUE

When the springtime had come, the young man, girded tightly up at the waist, stood on the high cliff and looked ecstatically at the breaking up of the ice. The wind rippled the skirts of his coat and caressed his pale, glowing cheeks.

The air was still cold; however the sun had already risen halfway in the sky to herald the approaching spring: away from here... —away from here, far away, to the unknown land; there, beyond the endless sea...!

And he sat on the rock, took a pen, and with numbed frozen fingers wrote his heart's song to the spring—which no one understood—and his soul enjoyed this song.

And when the summer came, he walked amidst the seashore foliage searching for roses. He gathered up violets, putting them in his buttonhole, telling his story and singing to them.

But when the autumn came, he girded himself again and walked the streets, looking at the flowers of asphalt on wet streets and singing his song to the autumn: The sea of light and souls, filled with Destinies...!

Yellow leaves fluttered down, clung to the ground or rolled in gutters. The wheels of cars squelched, making shadows run, bound to them. Nobody hung around on the sidewalks, but hurriedly they all walked on, the long spikes of umbrellas clicking on each other now and then.

The young man walked slowly, searching. He searched for the voice of his heart in the night, wanting to sing his whole song. Because his fantasy was: to be allowed to breathe, and just to be and to sing, because the chance of birth had created him.

He lived and sung his song to the very end. When winter and coldness came, he froze to death!

—What was the purpose of his life? And what did he search for?
We do not know!?

But there is in the cemetery a grave with a name on the cross, and it, like the other graves, is sheltered by high spruces. And in summertime flowers bloom on this grave as well as on the other graves!

This story, entitled "An Unknown Poet," was written in 1930 by my old wise friend when he was only 23 years old. Flowers have bloomed on his grave already for many, many years. This story has always deeply moved me in its utter simplicity, clumsiness, and its dream-like innocence. It is not high-brow, clever, or intelligent, but it is illuminated by the light of the heart, reflecting truthfully what human life is in a wider context. It is not an optimistic story, nor pessimistic, neither valuable nor worthless, but something enormously immense, boundless, something which contains all opposites, all lights and shades of the mystery of life.

I have now, in my own way, from my own place in life, written one dream book for my contemporaries, which will be read fleetingly by some, and then sink like a thousand other dream books into the ocean of oblivion. Between the lines of this dream book, the same autumn song of the young poet is heard, hardly audible at times.

I present my acknowledgements to my contemporaries who have made this book possible with their dreams. My deepest gratitude to my Dream Master, Montague Ullman, for the keys to the dream world, for his warm humor, and his tremendous ability to listen to his fellow man. How could I leave unsaid my devoted thanks to my wife, Pirjo Juhela, whose sharp-sighted critique of my text proved to be excruciatingly pertinent and accurate, time after time elevating my scribbles to a readable manuscript, and to my son Markus for his wholehearted support for this book project.

My very deep gratitude and special thanks to Richard Jenkins, who unexpectedly and spontaneously made an offer to proofread my manuscript translation to English. His keen perception and insight about my actual ideas behind my clumsy translation, which needed two thousand corrections, has helped me more than I could even *dream* of.

MARKKU SIIVOLA, SPRING 2011

ENDNOTES

1   Buber, Martin. *I and Thou*. New York: Charles Scribner's Sons, 1970.

2   James, William. *Principles of Psychology, Vols. 1 & 2*. New York: Cosimo Classics, 2007.

3   Translation from the Finnish poem To Youth by Orvo Raippamaa.

4   Gardiner, Alan H. *Hieratic Papyri in the British Museum, 3rd Series*. Chester Beatty Gift. "Papyrus No.III: The Dream Book" [Papyrus Facsimile + text and annotations]. British Museum: London, 1935.

5   Parsifal-Charles, Nancy. *The Dream: 4.000 Years of Theory and Practice*. Locust Hill Press: Stephen's Church, 1986.

6   Artemidorus. *Oneirocritica (The Interpretation of Dreams)*. Park Ridge: Noyes Press, 1975.

7   Pontalis, J.B. "Dream as an object." *International Journal of Psychoanalysis*. 1974.

8   Pontalis, J.B. *Frontiers in Psychoanalysis*. London: Hogarth Press, 1981.

9   Tähkä, Veikko. *Mind and Its Treatment: A Psychoanalytic Approach*. Madison: International Universities Press, 1993.

10   Freud, Sigmund. "Resistance and Repression." Lecture XIX. Wien Lectures, 1915-1917.

11   Hesse, Hermann. *The Glass Bead Game*. New York: Holt, Rinehart & Winston, 1969. From the Preface of the Finnish translation, *Lasihelmipeli* by Kai Laitinen. Helsinki: Kirjayhtymä, 1978.

12   Ullman, Montague. "Dream Interpretation vs. Dream Appreciation." Dream Appreciation Newsletter. 3 (1998). http://siivola.org/monte/Dream_Appreciation_Newsletter/1998-3.pdf.

13   Fromm, Erich. *The Forgotten Language: An Introduction to the Understanding of Dreams, Fairy Tales, and Myths*. New York: Holt, Rinehart & Winston, 1951.

14 Ullman, Montague. "The Orchestration—Letting the Dream Speak." *Dream Appreciation.* 3 (1998).

15 Reiser, Morton. "The Dream in Contemporary Psychiatry." *American Journal of Psychiatry.* 158 (2001).

16 Einstein, Albert. *The World As I See It.* New York: Philosophical Library, 1949.

17 Whitman, Walt. *Leaves of Grass.* Brooklyn, 1855.

18 Freud, Sigmund. Quotation from 1895 recorded by Library of Congress, [published 1950]. "Conflict, Freud, & Culture." http://www.loc.gov/exhibits/freud/ex/22.html.

19 Freud, Sigmund. "The Question of a Weltanschauung." Lecture XXXV. *New Introductory Lectures on Psychoanalysis.* New York: W.W. Norton, 1932.

20 Freud, Sigmund. *New Introductory Lectures on Psychoanalysis.* New York: W.W. Norton, 1932.

21 Gay, Peter. *Freud: A Life for our Time.* New York: W.W. Norton, 1988.

22 Jung, C.G. *Memories, Dreams, Reflections.* New York: Random House, 1961.

23 Fromm, Erich. *Greatness and Limitations of Freud's Thought.* New York: New American Library, 1980.

24 Jung, C.G. "Children's Dreams: Notes from the Seminar Given in 1936-1940 (Jung Seminars)." C. G. Jung, Lorenz Jung, Maria Meyer-Grass, Ernst Falzeder, Tony Woolfson. "SEMINAR 1 Professor Jung: On the Method of Dream Interpretation." 25 October 1938.

25 Ullman, Montague. "Reflections on Life Inside and Outside a Dream Group." Dream Appreciation Newsletter. 4 (1999).

26 Jung, C.G. *Über die Psychologie des Unbewussten.* Frankfurt: Fisher, 1960.

27 Perls, Frederick S. *Gestalt Therapy Verbatim.* Boulder: Real People Press, 1969.

28 Sontag, Susan. *Against Interpretation.* New York: Dell, 1966.

29 Hillman, James. *The Dream and the Underworld.* New York: Harper & Row, 1979.

30 Marozza, Maria Ilena. "When does a dream begin to 'have meaning'?" *Journal of Analytical Psychology.* 50 (2005): 693–705.

31 Freud, Sigmund. *A General Introduction to Psychoanalysis.* New York: Boni & Liveright, 1920.

32 Gay, Peter. *Freud: A Life for our Time.* New York: W.W. Norton, 1988.

33 Freud, Sigmund. *New Introductory Lectures on Psychoanalysis*. New York: W.W. Norton, 1932.

34 Jung, C.G. *Memories, Dreams, Reflections*. New York: Random House, 1961.

35 Salminen, Heimo. *Ihminen on kuin valo—Medard Boss*. Helsinki: Weilin & Göös, 1980.

36 Ullman, Montague. "Interconnectedness: Species Unity and Dreaming." *Dream Appreciation*. 5 (2000).

37 Revonsuo, A. "The reinterpretation of dreams: An evolutionary hypothesis of the function of dreaming." *Behavioral and Brain Sciences*. 23 (2000): 877–901.

38 Translated from: Orvo Raippamaa's Henkinen johtaja meissä.

39 Jung, C.G. "Approaching the Unconscious." *Man and His Symbols*. Menlo Park: Aldus Books, 1964.

40 Freud, Sigmund. "The Philosophy of a Life Source." Lecture XXXV. *New Introductory Lectures on Psychoanalysis*. London: Hogarth Press, 1933.

41 Jung, C.G. *Memories, Dreams, Reflections*. New York: Random House, 1961.

42 Harrison, Jim. *Just Before Dark*. New York: Houghton Mifflin, 1991.

43 Kilpi, Volter. Ihmisestä ja elämästä. 1902. Transkirjan uusintapainos, 1990.

44 Kilpi, Volter. Varhaiset kertomukset. 1901–1903. Volter Kilven seura, 1990.

45 Kilpi, Volter. Alastalon salissa. osa II. 1933.

46 Kilpi, Volter. Merimiehen leski. Kirjassa: Pitäjän pienempiä, 1934.

47 Ullman, Montague. *Appreciating Dreams—A Group Approach*. New York: Cosimo Books, 2006.

48 Blake, William. *Auguries of Innocence*. New York: Grossman Publishers 1968.

49 Fromm, Erich. *The Forgotten Language: An Introduction to the Understanding of Dreams, Fairy Tales, and Myths*. New York: Holt, Rinehart & Winston, 1951.

50 Ullman, Montague. "The Experiential Dream Group." *Handbook of Dreams—Research, Theories and Applications*. Benjamin B. Wolman, Montague Ullman, and Wilse B. Webb, eds. New York: Van Nostrand Reinhold, 1979.

51 Jung, C.G. *On the Nature of Dreams*. Zurich: Rascher, 1948.

52 Matthew 7:2. New King James Bible.

53 Ullman Montague. "The Bindelof Story." Exceptional Human *Experience*. 11–13 (1993–1995). www.siivola.org/monte/papers_grouped/copyrighted/Parapsychology_&_Psi/Bindelof_Story/index.htm.

54 Einstein, Albert. *Ideas and Opinions*. New York: Crown Publishing, 1954.

55   Goldman, Robert N. *Einstein's God—Albert Einstein's Quest as a Scientist and as a Jew to Replace a Forsaken God.* Northvale: Joyce Aronson, Inc., 1997.

56   Hadamard, Jacques. *The Psychology of Invention in the Mathematical Field.* Education in Vision Series. Princeton, 1943.

57   Ullman, Montague. "On the Relevance of Quantum Concepts to Dreaming Consciousness." Date unknown, between 2001-2005.

58   Bohm, David. *Wholeness and the Implicate Order.* London: Routledge, 1980.

59   Ullman, Montague. "Wholeness and Dreaming." *Quantum Implications: Essays in honor of David Bohm.* B.J. Hiley and F. David Peat, eds. London: Routledge; New York: Kegan Paul, 1987.

60   Ullman, Montague. "The Transformation Process In Dreams." 79 (1975). Conference of Scientists with J. Krishnamurti. American Academy of Psychoanalysis. Brockwood Park. 14 Oct. 1974.

61   Lutyens, Mary. *Krishnamurti—The Years of Awakening.* Avon Books: New York, 1976.

62   Jung, C.G. *Memories, Dreams, Reflections.* New York: Random House, 1961.

INDEX

ABOUT THE AUTHOR

As a young man, MARKKU SIIVOLA (b. 1945) was convinced he would become a chemist, but after mystical experiences in his twenties, his main interest became the human psyche. He switched to medicine and specialized in psychiatry. A major part of his career was in liaison and rehabilitation psychiatry in Finland and Sweden.

In 1980, he participated in a dream group for the first time, led by Dr. Montague Ullman in Sweden. It became a pivotal point in his life. Since then he has led groups for non-professionals and professionals. Siivola is an approved dream group leader and supervisor in Sweden, and in 2008 he was nominated as an honorary member of the Swedish Dream Group Forum. He is the co-founder of the Finnish Dream Group Forum, founded in 2003. He created Montague Ullman's website in 1999 and later developed the Swedish Dream Group Forum site.

He translated Ullman's book Working with Dreams into Finnish in 1982. Siivola wrote and compiled the first detailed instructions for the dream group process, published by the University of Jyvaskyla in 1984. It was expanded into the bestselling Unien Opissa in 2008, now used throughout Finland by dream group enthusiasts as their main textbook. You can find him online at *www.saunalahti.fi/msiivola/*.

COSIMO is a specialty publisher of books and publications that inspire, inform, and engage readers. Our mission is to offer unique books to niche audiences around the world.

COSIMO BOOKS publishes books and publications for innovative authors, nonprofit organizations, and businesses.

COSIMO BOOKS specializes in bringing books back into print, publishing new books quickly and effectively, and making these publications available to readers around the world.

COSIMO CLASSICS offers a collection of distinctive titles by the great authors and thinkers throughout the ages.

At **COSIMO CLASSICS** timeless works find new life as affordable books, covering a variety of subjects including: Business, Economics, History, Personal Development, Philosophy, Religion & Spirituality, and much more!

COSIMO REPORTS publishes public reports that affect your world, from global trends to the economy, and from health to geopolitics.

FOR MORE INFORMATION CONTACT US AT
INFO@COSIMOBOOKS.COM

> ➤ if you are a book lover interested in our current catalog of books

> ➤ if you represent a bookstore, book club, or anyone else interested in special discounts for bulk purchases

> ➤ if you are an author who wants to get published

> ➤ if you represent an organization or business seeking to publish books and other publications for your members, donors, or customers.

**COSIMO BOOKS ARE ALWAYS
AVAILABLE AT ONLINE BOOKSTORES**

VISIT COSIMOBOOKS.COM
BE INSPIRED, BE INFORMED

Lightning Source UK Ltd.
Milton Keynes UK
UKOW030612171111

182219UK00001B/2/P